## West Indies

'I have enjoyed your fine single malt for some time now.
I was introduced to it **by a friend in the medical profession** in the UK.'

## France

'Please find enclosed my coupon for a certificate
of property of a square foot of the island of Islay.
As further proof of purchase
**I enclose a whiff of my breath.**'

## Norway

'Since my first taste of Laphroaig in 1988,
many good friends have had the benefit of enjoying
a dram of Laphroaig in my house. It is essential, however,
**to give all enjoyers their first lesson** –
how to smell and taste a dram of Laphroaig.'

1815 - 2015
# 200
## YEARS OF
# LAPHROAIG®

# 1815 - 2015
# 200
## YEARS OF
## LAPHROAIG®

Marcel van Gils & Hans Offringa

# Table of Contents

# Foreword

When Hans Offringa and Marcel van Gils asked me to write the foreword for their book, they certainly addressed the Islay resident more than the whisky writer. Living by the shore, away from pollution and noise, it is my privilege to inhale a pure briny air. On a full moon night, I can admire the silvery staircase the 'man in the moon' draws on the surface of the water. On a wintery gale day, I can stand against the waves on a pier, amidst the elements, almost getting a taste of a medicinal and peated Islay malt from the sea!

Islay distilleries are a constituent element of Islay, as much as Islay nature has carved each individual whisky. This is why Laphroaig encapsulates the marine fragrances of the air, releasing a combination of smoke and iodine. As the authors state, Laphroaig is built on three pillars: the art of distillation, the ancient soil of Islay and its people, the Ileachs.

Who better than a talented whisky writer and an erudite Laphroaig collector could bring to light the secrets of the iconic Islay single malt? Hans and Marcel started their journey of discovery into Laphroaig history in 2007 when they produced *The Legend of Laphroaig,* a book which gives a comprehensive account of the distillery past. They searched the archives, uncovering fascinating documents and old photos.

One could think that all has been told about 'the hollow by the fine bay'. But the two friends have done it again, taking a different approach this time. If they have used some of the material from the first book, especially the genealogy facts they dug up from different archives, they have focused on the people for *200 Years of Laphroaig 1815-2015.* They have found retired distillers and interviewed them. They also have met the actual team - from the maltmen through to the visitors centre - and individually portrayed them, thus demonstrating that people are a major ingredient in the making of a good whisky. They have also featured the Friends of Laphroaig, the whisky lovers who spread the good word all around the world.

Superbly illustrated, offering an accurate and rich insight into two hundred years of the life of a legendary whisky, this book is a milestone in the memory of Laphroaig and a definitive, heartfelt contribution to knowledge. Knowledge is a source of enjoyment. This is why, immersed in reading *200 Years of Laphroaig*, a dram by its side, the reader will enjoy the medicinal flavours of his favourite Laphroaig even better.

'No half measures; love it or hate it', Laphroaig advertising proclaims. That reminds me of St Augustine's quote: 'The measure of love is to love without measure'. This is exactly what Hans Offringa and Marcel van Gils have done: tell the story of a whisky to be loved without measure.

*Martine Nouet - Islay, November 2015*

# Origins

# Origins

Laphroaig is built on three pillars: the millennia old art of distillation, the ancient soil of a small Hebridean island and last but not least, the salt of the earth – The Ileachs, as the inhabitants of the Isle of Islay prefer to call themselves. For generations the Johnstons, MacAffers, MacDougalls, McDonalds, Campbells, McTaggarts, McIntyres, Gilchrists, Grahams and the likes have put their hand to making fine whisky at the beautiful spot where the distillery is located. Various descendants of these proud families currently work at the distillery. You will meet some of these people later in this story. First we will have a look at the other two pillars that have contributed to what Laphroaig is today.

## Distillation

The origins of distilling are misty and unclear. Over time stories have been written down by a variety of historians, journalists and amateurs. Each individual author claims his or her story to be true. We don't, but we have tried to come as close to the truth as possible. One favourite tale is that of distillation coming from China and travelling via India to the Middle East. The old silk route of Marco Polo might have been the route through which the knowledge travelled. There is no solid evidence available to sustain this theory.

What we do know is that rudimentary distilling equipment was found in Mesopotamia (roughly the current Iraq area) in the 1980s. Scientists ware able to date it to 3500 BC. The equipment consists of a clay pot and a collecting ring. The former can hold forty litres, the latter about two. It can be described as a very primitive still, but must have been unsuitable for whisky distilling as we know it today. The main purpose might have been to extract scents that could be put to use in balms and essences.

It would take a few millennia before written references to distilled beverages surfaced. In India a fierce liquor called 'arrack' was recorded around 800 BC. It would probably have been made of fermented rice or cane juice. When the famous Greek philosopher Aristotle (384-322 BC) described the process of salt being gained from seawater, he unwittingly witnessed a natural form of distillation, the sun evaporating the water, leaving the salt on the beach.

St Patrick (387-461), who made a career from slave to bishop, is often credited with bringing distillation to Ireland, whilst spreading Christianity. Another famous spiritual leader, Irish-born St Columba, would then have followed in his footsteps more than a century later, bringing distillation to Scotland when he set foot on Iona in 563. From there he made many travels back to Ireland and to the Scottish mainland, even visiting Glasgow before his death in 597. On the Kintyre peninsula one can find a footprint that is attributed to St Columba. He must have had large feet.

If St Patrick really did know about distilling, how might he have acquired that knowledge? Egypt could have been a realistic source. Queen Cleopatra (69-30 BC) knew about distillation and used it among other purposes for manufacturing makeup. The Arabic word *al-kohl* referred to a fine black powder used as a cosmetic. Her famous lover and Roman commander Marc Anthony might have been the transmitter to Rome, from where the knowledge was spread over Europe to eventually end up in Britain. This leads to speculation whether the Scots already knew their dram when St Columba arrived at Iona. Probably the Irish will immediately protest against such a theory, pointing out that Hadrian's Wall (built around 120 AD) prevented distilling coming via England into Scotland. Although Ireland never belonged to the Roman Empire, found coins and pottery give evidence of contact with the Romans, both via trading and raids on the Irish coast. Following that line of reasoning, a passing of distillation techniques from Rome to Ireland is plausible. Interesting theories but they might be qualified as urban legends, lacking clear evidence, especially in the light of what happened a couple of centuries later in the Middle East. Events that were documented accurately.

It took more than 4,000 years from the times that the little clay pot in Mesopotamia was used until written references to distillation techniques showed up in the works of Islamic scholars, most notably those of Geber, Al-Razi and Avicenna. Geber (721-815), whose full name was Abu Musa Jabir ibn Hayyan, was a Renaissance-man *avant la lettre*, not only a well-known physicist, but also a gifted astronomer, alchemist and philosopher. In Europe he is considered to be the father of Arab chemistry. Geber did groundbreaking work in turning alchemy from magic into real science and is credited for many inventions that would form the basis of several tools used in laboratories today. One of them is the alembic, of which the copper pot stills in many distilleries are a modern form. Some historians claim an earlier and simpler form of the alembic was already invented around 200-300, either by Maria the Jewess or Zósimo and Teosebeia of Panoplies.

Geber was not primarily interested in distilling alcohol. He observed a flammable vapour when distilling, but ultimately tried to create an elixir (from the Arabic *al-iksr*) that could turn one metal into another, preferably lead into gold. Geber described the vapour as 'of little use, but of great importance to science'. Al-Razi (864-930) made references to alcohol as a medicine. Avicenna (10th century) is reputed to be the first to have used steam distillation. He distilled a mixture of water and rose petals, thus creating the first perfume of modern times. The Moors might have taken distilling from Arabia to Spain, where the art was embraced by monasteries and widely spread over Western Europe.

Several of Geber's writings were translated into Latin, such as *the Kitab al-Kimya* into *The Book of the Composition of Alchemy* (1144) by Robert of Chester. Medieval European scholars used these early writings enthusiastically and concentrated on making alcoholic beverages for medicinal purposes. Michael Scott (1175-1234) was the first West European scholar and 'magician' to define technical distilling terms instead of alchemy in his work *Lumen Luminem*, published in 1225. He taught at the medical school of Salerno, Italy.

Arnoldus Villanova might have picked up distilling on its way to Britain in 1290 when he wrote the first manual on the subject, while teaching medicine at the university of Montpellier in France. Around the same time the French Bethunes, a famous family of physicians, manifested themselves in Ireland and Scotland as MacBeth or MacBheata (Beaton in England). Patrick MacBeth was medical advisor to King Robert I (the Bruce) of Scotland in the 14th century and Rory MacBetha was one of the first to be physician to the Lord of the Isles.

The MacBheatas were famous throughout Britain and possessed a huge library of medical books in Gaelic, translated from original Arabic and Greek manuscripts. Since distillation had gradually become the domain of the medical profession, they must have had a thorough knowledge about the process. One of the MacBeths, Ferchard or Fergus, was given the Isle of Jura in 1386 as a thank you from Robert II of Scotland. Fergus branched out to Kilchoman on Islay, which fact can be proved by a commemorating cross dating from the late 14th century. Legend has it that the MacBheatas originally came to Scotland in 1300 via Ireland with Princess Agnes who married Angus Og Macdonald, Lord of the South Isles, a personal friend of Robert the Bruce. This branch of the MacBheatas first settled in Kintyre but quickly moved to Islay. From the Mull of Kintyre to Kildalton on Islay is a mere 15 miles as the crow flies.

The first recordings of distillation in Ireland come from a rather obscure source, called *The Red Book of Ossory*. It is assumed to have been compiled in the 14th century by an Irish bishop named Richard Ledred. The first complete illustrated book on distillation in Europe was written by Hieronymus Braunschweig (or Brunswyck), a German scholar, in 1507. Laurence Andrew translated it into English in 1527.

The first written record on whisky in Scotland appears almost 200 years later in 1494 and has been quoted many times: 'To Friar John Cor, by order of the King, to make aqua vitae VIII bols of malt.' Cor was from Lindores Abbey in the eastern Lowlands. At the time distillation was primarily done by monks, who used alcohol as medicine for a variety of diseases. When King Henry VIII decided to create his own form of Church, he was excommunicated by the Pope in Rome. He saw this as a great offense and took revenge on the Roman Catholics in Britain by demolishing monasteries, selling lands the Church had owned to his cronies and putting monks out on the streets. In order to survive they had to find the odd job wherever they could. Many of them ended up as farm hands. To make themselves more useful, they might have taught the art of distilling to their employer.

As early as the 16th century, farmers distilled whisky from a portion of their grain crops. Generally to make a bit of extra money and to extract some value from a wet harvest. The fuel for the stills was right next door and, not unimportantly, free: the farmer went outside and struck his own peat, ubiquitous in the Highlands and on the islands. Another advantage in the countryside was the relative inaccessibility, especially on remote islands like Islay and in the Highlands – an illegal still could be hidden much easier in a remote glen than in a busy city street. Whisky is

*Tallant Farm around 1900.*

made using great quantities of water, hence the proximity of clear spring water was a necessity. Close to the source clearly meant close to nature as well. Between the 17th and 19th century a true cottage industry of farm distilleries developed, with each one making his own specific single malt. There was hardly any export to the Lowlands or England, since the southern neighbours of the Highlanders considered its whiskies too distinctive in taste. They preferred brandy (cognac) or gin instead.

During the 19th century, six important events would reshape the entire Scottish whisky landscape and in its wake the drinking preferences of the English.

The first event was the passing of the Excise Act in 1823. This law made it possible to acquire a distilling license against relatively little cost. Within a couple of years most illicit distillers followed suit and single malts became easier to acquire. Many current day legitimate distillers are located on sites once used illicitly. This may be one of the reasons that we only see Laphroaig registered as an official brand, or trademark if you prefer, in 1826. No distiller in his right mind would have gone to the registrar's office before 1824 to report he was doing something illegal!

The second event was an Irish invention. In 1827 distiller Robert Stein patented a still type that was capable of distilling continuously. It was no pot still as used by the Scottish Highlanders but a column. Another Irishman, Aeneas Coffey, improved the still and registered it in 1830.

The column still, also called Coffey still, was born and from that moment it was possible to distil whisky on a grand industrial scale. Remarkably the Irish found the column still far too modernistic and decided against it. Not the Scots, especially the Lowlanders. They immediately applied the new still to produce a cheaper, more neutral kind of whisky than the distinctive and more expensive malt whiskies from the Highlands and the Islands.

The third event was the repeal of the Corn Laws in 1846. Before that year distillers were only allowed to use barley to make whisky.

From then on other types of grain could be used too, like maize (corn) and wheat, both also being cheaper. Companies that use the column still to make whisky from the latter two grains are called grain distillers.

The fourth event was a change of law in Scotland around 1860. Till then blending distillates from different grains was prohibited. It was Andrew Usher who saw a huge possibility here and he is considered the father of whisky blending. Usher bought casks containing single malts from individual malt distillers and blended those with the cheaper grain alcohol or grain whisky. He also blended various single malts and called the end product 'Usher's Old Vatted Glenlivet Malt Whisky'. Soon grocers and wine merchants, traditionally the ones buying and selling whisky, followed his example. In Aberdeen the Chivas brothers started blending; in Perth, John Dewar and Alexander Bell joined the blending band. William Teacher started in Glasgow and elsewhere Johnnie Walker, George Ballantine, Robert Haig and James Buchanan learned the art of blending. The majority of these names still live on in famous Scottish blends. There is also a famous blend connected to Laphroaig, called Islay Mist.

The fifth event happened on the European continent. In 1863 France was confronted with a disaster that would decimate the French vineyards within a few decades. This was caused by a mean little creature called *Phylloxera vastatrix*, a minute aphidlike insect that lives on grape roots and foliage, accidentally imported from the USA. The French couldn't make cognac anymore and the English began to miss their brandy. As a replacement they turned to blended whisky from Scotland. It was an instant success and the Highlanders regarded that development with suspicious eyes and minds, wanting to protect their single malts. At the turn of the century a true economic whisky boom had developed and some blenders weren't too concerned about the – lack of – quality of their product.

The sixth event took place in 1898. The notorious Pattison brothers caused a huge crisis in the Scottish whisky industry when they were caught doctoring the whisky as well as their books. They were put behind bars and unwittingly became instrumental in the early 20th century discussion 'What is Whisky', ending in a change of the law in 1917 describing production specifications to a T. One of the stipulations stated that whisky must mature in oak casks for a minimum of three years and has to be at least 40% ABV when bottled.

Blended whisky performed well outside Scotland and England as a replacement drink for cognac. When famous Hollywood stars such as Humphrey Bogart and Dean Martin openly enjoyed the pleasures of blended Scotch, the export of the drink rose sky high. Blends continue to play a major role everywhere in the world. Since Laphroaig is well liked by blenders, there might be a drop of it in your favourite blend.

Around 1990 the market share of single malt whisky started to grow and has done ever since. The last three decades have seen a huge upsurge of single malts worldwide and Laphroaig can be found in many bars around the globe. The Friends of Laphroaig, a loyalty program launched by former distillery manager Iain Henderson and marketeer Jeremy Weatherhead, has been running since 1994 and can boast over 700,000 Friends. Chapter 5 is exclusively dedicated to this phenomenon. Each Friend 'owns' a square foot of Islay, the ancient island on which the distillery, started on a farm two centuries ago, proudly stands. So, what about the origins of that island?

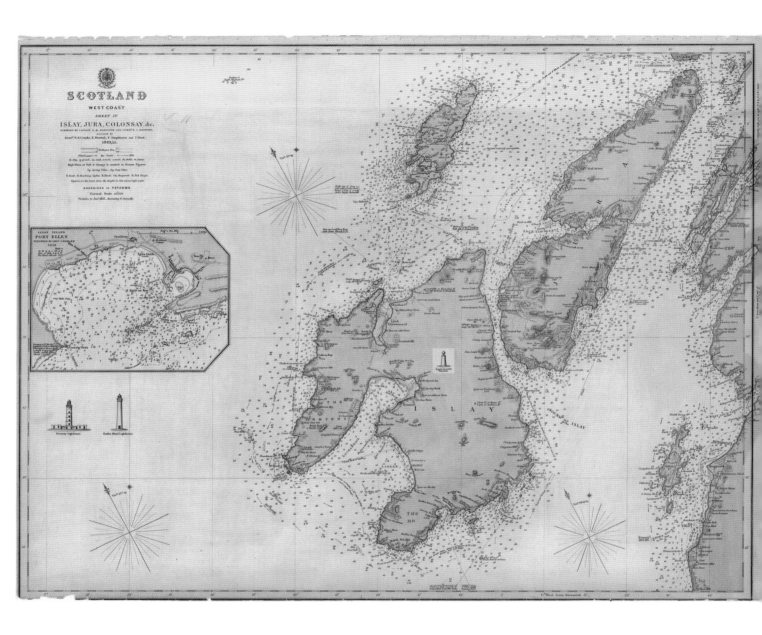

## The Isle of Islay

Scientists estimate the age of the earth at about 4.5 billion years. What is now known as Scotland, was originally an enormous land mass called Laurentia, stretching out to Greenland and North America. Around 4.5 million years ago it collided with two other gigantic land masses named Baltica and Avalonia, each consisting of different types of stone. As a result Scotland was divided into several faults with their own geological characteristics.

Islay itself was formed some 60 million years ago after a long series of volcanic eruptions. Some surface stones even date back to half the age of the earth: at Portnahaven pebbles of Lewisian gneiss can be found in the little bay that is a natural shelter for seals. On the other side of the island, at Ardnave Point, one can find surface rock of a similar age.

The first traces of human habitation on Islay originated 10,000 years ago, after the last minor ice age. At the time the climate was milder and Islay would probably have been more wooded than today. Mesolithic fishermen and hunters entered the island by boat from the mainland. These nomadic people became settlers around 3500 BC, when the Neolithic period commenced. Evidence is found in remains of pottery and stone axes for felling trees. When the farming population grew, the people commenced building burial tombs with cairns on top of them. These multi-chambered graves can be found in several places, most notably in Port Charlotte and at Cragabus in The Oa.

Standing stones appeared at the end of the Neolithic period. The Cultoon Stone Circle, built between 2500-1500 BC might have been an early astronomical device. It can be found between Portnahaven and Kilchiaran and seems to have never been fully erected, abandoned during construction. Cultoon is one of the latest known stone circles, at a time when they were going out of fashion. During this period the climate gradually changed. It became wetter and colder, moorlands developed and heavy rainfall caused the forming of many peat bogs.

In the Iron Age Islay was littered with small fortresses, being a battleground for many an armed argument. Stone hill forts like Dun Nosebridge in the Laggan Valley probably date back to 400 BC. Around 400 (AD) Christianity came to Islay, brought by Irish monks. They built little chapels everywhere, divided over tiny parishes with names like Kilnave and Kildalton, which each had their own burial ground. The word 'kil' is derived from the Gaelic 'cill' meaning church. In the next couple of ages beautiful stone crosses were erected in the so-called Iona-tradition.

The Kildalton Cross, a fine example of this style, richly decorated with Celtic, Pictish, Northumbrian and Irish motifs, dates back to 800. Around that time the Viking raiders began to pester the Islay coast. The clergy retreated to Ireland and left the population to fend for itself. On the one hand the Norse and Danish intruders were extremely cruel. Excavations under the Kildalton Cross showed the remains of a body that was 'blood-eagled', a favourite pastime of the Vikings.

A captive, usually a chief, would be tied to the ground on his belly. Then his lungs and heart were torn out and spread on his back. This horrible punishment was supposed to be an 'honour' only bestowed upon great warriors. On the other hand the Norse slowly mixed with the indigenous Christians and were converted themselves. Evidence of the presence of the Vikings can be found in burial sites such as Cruach Mhor, located between Laggan Point and Islay Airport.

It is often said that the Ileachs truly differ from the Scots, which might have been caused by the fact that they were under Norse rule much longer than their Pictish and Scottish cousins on the mainland. Mid-12th century the Norse yoke was finally thrown off the Ileachs shoulders when Somerled, King of Argyll defeated the Norse at sea. He founded the MacDonald clan and chose Dunyvaig Castle as his residence. The remains of this fortress can still be seen in Lagavulin Bay, a stone's throw from Laphroaig.

Around the turn of the 13th century, Angus Og, a descendant of Somerled, rose to power. His son John acquired the title Lord of the Isles in 1336. From that date the Clan MacDonald ruled not only over Islay, but also over the Kintyre peninsula, Knapdale, Skye, Lewis and the Western part of Scotland. The Chiefs of Clan Donald chose Finlaggan at Eilean Mor, in the centre of the island, as the seat of power for the Lord of the Isles. The first Lord was also named Good John of Islay because he was a pious man and helped build many churches. His father modified the Great Seal of Islay, which is shown on the label of Islay Mist, the blend made with Laphroaig whisky at its core. In 1542 the title 'Lord of the Isles' was seized by the English Crown and held ever since.

The MacDonalds continued to rule this part of Scotland until 1542 when Donald Dubh (grandson of John II, the 4th Lord of the Isles) lost a rebellion. The Campbells of Cawdor seized power and eventually took Dunyvaig from the MacDonalds, who had owned the castle for more than 450 years. The remains of the Finlaggan stronghold of Clan Donald can still be seen on Eilean Mor and are in the custody of the Finlaggan Trust.

In the early 17th century the Scottish king gave the entire isle of Islay to Sir John Campbell of Cawdor, who managed to defeat the MacDonalds definitively a couple of years later. Islay would slowly become more and more a part of Scotland. The Cawdor Campbells weren't too successful in ruling Islay. They were hardly ever there, preferring to stay in Argyll. There was one exception to that rule, Sir Hugh Campbell, who erected Islay House around 1680. Eventually it became a burden for his successor John Campbell who ran into a financial disaster and had to sell Islay to Daniel, a member of the Shawfield branch of clan Campbell.

The Shawfield Campbells brought great prosperity to Islay and were responsible for building many roads and villages such as Bowmore with its famous round church. Bowmore is built on a rectangular grid with wide streets. At the time this was a novelty. The eponymous distillery is the oldest on Islay, dating back to 1779. It is currently owned by Suntory, who bought Beam Global in 2014, thus joining Bowmore and Laphroaig at the Japanese hip, so to speak.

Let's not run ahead, but return to the late 18th century. When Daniel Campbell the Younger died in 1777, his brother Walter Campbell succeeded him from Skipness. The population grew from an estimated 5,000 in 1755 to more than 8,000 in 1801 when the first official census on Islay was held.

In 1816 Daniel Campbell's grandson Walter Frederick Campbell inherited Islay, a year after Laphroaig claims to have been founded. Campbell initiated many changes on the island, of which several were so influential that they can still be noted today, mainly in housing and farming. The population continued to prosper and grow until coming to a grinding halt around 1845, partly caused by overpopulation (15,000 inhabitants), partly by the potato disease from neighbouring Ireland. Clearances took place, forcing many people off the island, to make room for sheep. Walter Frederick Campbell faced a huge financial crisis and his affairs were handed to a trust. His son John Francis Campbell dealt with the creditors and was assisted by John Ramsay, a local farmer and distiller.

John Ramsay was a remarkable man. Born in Glasgow in 1815, he went to Islay at age 18 and took the position of manager at Port Ellen Distillery. Over time he would befriend the then owner of Islay, Walter Frederick Campbell of Shawfield. The latter was impressed by the young man and offered him a job as financial advisor.

In 1855 Ramsay managed to buy the Kildalton parish and in later years acquired other parts of the island, thus becoming a landlord in his own right. Between 1867 and 1869 he built Kildalton House. Ramsay was active in politics too, as an MP for Stirling and anything but an absentee owner. He cared deeply for the Ileach and finished various projects Campbell had started, such as the high road from Port Ellen to Bowmore, the quay in Port Ellen harbour and various schools where the Gaelic speaking population could gain a knowledge of the English language. Ramsay also stimulated people to voluntarily emigrate to Canada during the period that Islay became overcrowded. For some who could not afford it themselves, he would pay passage. He really felt connected to these Ileachs and even visited them in Canada in 1870, to see how they fared. Aged 77, he passed away in 1892, in the library of his beloved Kildalton House.

Finally, in 1853 Islay was sold to James Morrison, a fortunate businessman, for £500,000. This purchase ended Islay's ownership by the Campbell clan. For the last Campbell who held Islay an obelisk was erected at Bridgend to commemorate what the Campbells had done for the island during their reign. Its inscription reads:

*John Francis Campbell of Islay. An eminent Celtic scholar, linguist, scientist and traveller. A true and patriotic Highlander. Loved alike by peer and peasant. By his 'Popular Tales of the West Highlands', 'Leabhar na Feinne' and other literary works, he preserved and rendered classic the folklore of the Scottish Highlands. He lies buried in Cannes in France. His memories live in the hearts of his countrymen. Born 1821- Died 1885.*

New owner English businessman James Morrison suffered from poor health at the time he acquired Islay and left business in the hands of his sons Alfred and Charles, the latter most prominently involved. John Ramsay managed to buy the Kildalton estate from the Morrisons in 1855, when they decided to sell limited parts of Islay. Charles Morrison died in his nineties. His nephew Hugh, son of Alfred, became the sole heir. Being married to a granddaughter of Walter Frederick Campbell, he coincidentally re-established a link to the Campbells of Shawfield.

The Morrison family sold off more parcels of their estate in years to come, but kept Islay House. In 1964, James Morrison's great-grandson John Granville Morrison was created Lord Margadale. Eventually the Morrisons sold Islay House in 1985. The current head of the family is Alistair John, 3rd Lord Margadale and still connected to the Campbells, via his great-grandmother.

Around 1835 more than 15,000 people inhabited Islay. Beginning with the clearances in the mid 1850's the population slowly declined to today's number of approximately 3,228 (2011 census). The Ileachs share a surface of 62,017 hectares and eight working distilleries. Most estates that were once owned by the Campbells and made up all of Islay are now in the hands of a small group of individuals.

The Campbell and Ramsay names continue to surface in the history of Laphroaig. Donald and Alexander Johnston, the founders, had become tenants under laird Walter Frederick Campbell. Donald's son Dugald was tenant under John Ramsay. Dugald's sisters Mary and Margaret were both married to a Campbell. Ian Hunter, great-nephew of the founders, inherited the distillery from his parents and eventually bought the property from Captain Iain Ramsay, son of John Ramsay. Hunter, who died childless, left his belongings, including the distillery to his secretary Bessie Williamson, who would later in life marry a Mr Wishart Campbell. The current distillery manager at Laphroaig is named... John Campbell.

The origins of the actual name of the distillery seem to be Norse – prudr-vik, meaning fine bay in English, might have been Gaelicised into Proaig/Phroaig. The addition of the Gaelic La (probably short for lag, meaning hollow) led to Laphroaig, which can best be translated as 'the hollow by the fine bay'. Over time the distillery name has been spelled differently as can be seen in various documents from the 19th century, so one might encounter Laphroig or Laphroag occasionally.

Now let's move on to the history of the distillery itself.

# The Distillery

# The Distillery

Pick up any distillery bottling of Laphroaig today and read the label carefully. Guaranteed, you will find a sentence reading 'Distilled and bottled in Scotland by D. Johnston & Co, Isle of Islay'. Although Laphroaig changed hands a couple of times between its inception in the early 19th century and today, all subsequent owners honoured the family name of the founders: Johnston.

Laphroaig states on its website and the neck label of its bottles that the distillery was established in 1815. Rent rolls, birth records and gravestone inscriptions on the island show that a sizeable number of Johnstons were already living on Islay before the Jacobite Rebellion of 1745. Alexander Johnston, who was almost certainly one of their descendants, married Mary Graham around 1783. They probably already farmed in the Kildalton area and are the parents of Donald and Alexander, who are credited with establishing Laphroaig Distillery. John Johnston, another descendant of the early 18th century Johnstons, was the son of Duncan Johnston and Catherine MacIntyre and a farmer/distiller at Tallant.

In 1826 John married Mary Johnston, a sister of Donald and Alexander. In all likelihood they were cousins. Through this marriage they united the Johnstons from Tallant and Kildalton. John and Mary are the parents of 'Sandy' Johnston. The latter would forge another bond between the two families later on by marrying Donald's daughter Isabella. The family tree on page 34-35 comes to the aid of those who want to keep track of who's who!

## Family Names

It is widely assumed that the Johnstons were from Maclain (MacDonald) stock and anglicised their name for safety reasons in the 17th century. In the past, various writers have tried to unravel the family history of the Johnstons. Mistakes were made, people were mixed up, cousins became brothers, fathers became sons. To the benefit of those authors it must be said that it wasn't an easy task to build a truthful family tree, since the early Johnstons had a special fondness for names like John, Donald, Alexander, Duncan, Mary and Isabella. Furthermore these earlier scribes didn't have access to such a powerful research tool as the internet.

When we researched material for *The Legend of Laphroaig*, published in 2007, an important source for *Laphroaig 1815-2015*, a different approach was chosen. After in-depth exploration of genealogy web archives, the results were compared with the distillery archives and what had been written in whisky books to date. Several discrepancies were found. The next step was to try finding direct descendants from both branches of the Laphroaig-Johnstons. The web provided several of them from the USA to Australia. Via email correspondence the final pieces of the puzzle could be put together.

Through the years the following theories have evolved. Some sources mention Glen Coe as the origin of the Johnstons of Laphroaig. This is based upon an old family legend, in which Bessie Williamson believed. You will meet her later. It told that the family's table linen was decorated with the crest of the Maclains of Glen Coe.

At the turn of the 15th century John Maclain of Ardnamurchan was appointed Bailie of Islay by King James IV. His task was to arrange the land tenure on the island that became known as the Maclain Extent. In dividing the land among tenants, John Maclain kept Corary, Island Farm, Tallant and the surrounding lands for himself. When Sir John Campbell became the owner of Islay in 1615, the Maclains were well established on the island. It might have been wiser to retain their support with land tenure, but instead Campbell tacksmen were granted tenancies in Corary, Tallant and surrounding areas. However, these lands reverted to the Johnstons between the mid-18th century and the 19th century. These Johnstons are considered to be descendants of John Maclain and his followers.

In 1625 the Maclains of Ardnamurchan were driven off their ancestral lands by Clan Campbell. They had no place to go and were scattered to the four winds. It is recorded that Maclains went to the Scottish Lowlands, Ireland, France and England. Some of them joined other clans such as the Camerons and the MacDonalds of Clan Ranald. Another group of Maclains moved from Ardnamurchan to the neighbouring islands of Coll and Tiree. When the Campbells became the owners of Islay in 1615, they needed help to develop the island. It is quite possible that some Maclains moved from Coll and Tiree to Islay at the turn of the 17th century. Around that time they may have decided to change their name to Johnston, having been evicted by the Campbells in earlier times.

A combination of the King James version and the Ardnamurchan version may be closest to the truth: John McIain might have created a solid base on Islay for the refugees of the ethnic cleansing in Ardnamurchan in the 17th century. Recent DNA research, conducted by the Maclain/MacKane Project seems to support the theory of the Johnstons being descendants of Clan Donald. DNA material of both Johnstons from Islay and MacDonalds from Ardnamurchan (who became known as the Maclains) show clear similarities. More research on this matter is being executed and may reveal the identity of the exact branch of Clan Donald from which the Islay Johnstons descend. Many members of the Johnston family are buried at Kilnaughton Cemetary.

In the first part of the 19th century, farming and distilling still went hand in hand. Tenants used part of the crops to make whisky and earned some extra money on the side. It was not unusual to use the distillate as a way of paying part of the rent to the laird, in this case Walter Frederick Campbell. He leased the areas known as Torradale and Tighcarmogan around Loch Laphroaig to Johnstons.

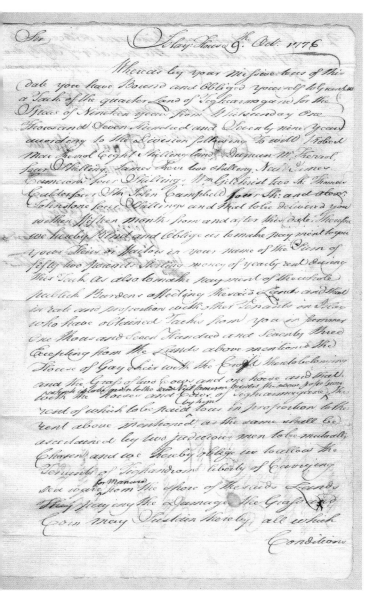

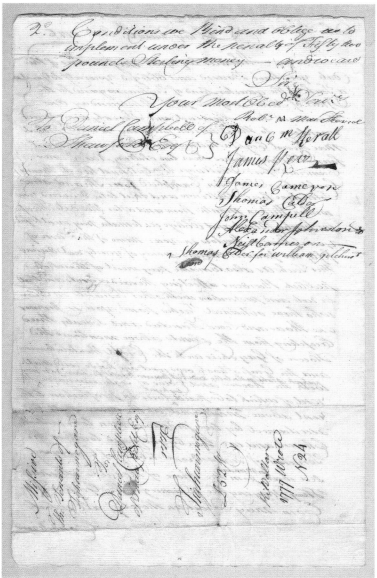

They are listed as tenants in rent rolls as early as 1776 and it is very likely Johnstons distilled there in 1815 or before, without a license. In an Information & Complaint bulletin of the Collector of Excise of Argyll, dated 17 February 1801, 'Sundries in the Island of Islay', various Johnstons are convicted for illicit distilling and retailing. Donald and Alexander Johnston are considered the official founders of Laphroaig Distillery. Donald, the entrepreneurial one of the two brothers, was initially recorded in the Excise accounts of 1826 as 'licensed distiller'.

The brothers might have come to the fore as legal distillers as a consequence of the 1823 change of law, which made it affordable to acquire a license. As usual the islands were lagging behind a few years in relation to 'lack of proximity' of government officials from London.

# The Johnston

## Tallant
### (and Corary)

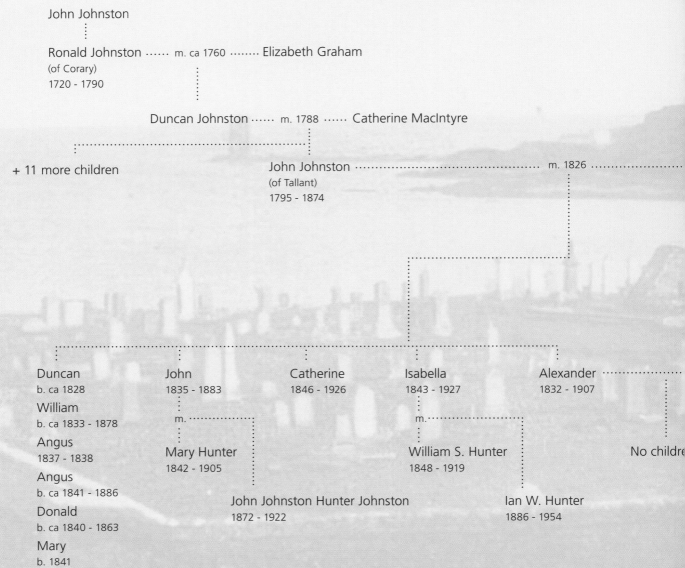

John Johnston

Ronald Johnston ······ m. ca 1760 ······ Elizabeth Graham
(of Corary)
1720 - 1790

Duncan Johnston ······ m. 1788 ······ Catherine MacIntyre

+ 11 more children

John Johnston ······································ m. 1826 ·····················
(of Tallant)
1795 - 1874

Duncan
b. ca 1828

William
b. ca 1833 - 1878

Angus
1837 - 1838

Angus
b. ca 1841 - 1886

Donald
b. ca 1840 - 1863

Mary
b. 1841

John
1835 - 1883

m. ········

Mary Hunter
1842 - 1905

John Johnston Hunter Johnston
1872 - 1922

Catherine
1846 - 1926

Isabella
1843 - 1927

m.

William S. Hunter
1848 - 1919

Ian W. Hunter
1886 - 1954

Alexander ··········
1832 - 1907

No childre

*b. born | m. married | d. died | bef. before*

# Family Tree

## Kildalton
### (Torradale and Tighcarmogan)

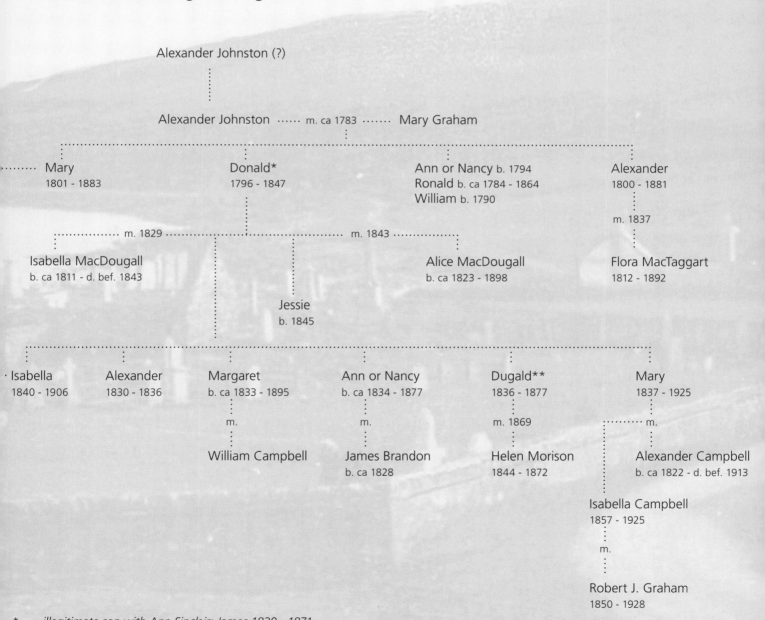

Alexander Johnston (?)

Alexander Johnston ······ m. ca 1783 ······ Mary Graham

Mary
1801 - 1883

Donald*
1796 - 1847

Ann or Nancy b. 1794
Ronald b. ca 1784 - 1864
William b. 1790

Alexander
1800 - 1881

m. 1837

······ m. 1829 ······

······ m. 1843 ······

Isabella MacDougall
b. ca 1811 - d. bef. 1843

Alice MacDougall
b. ca 1823 - 1898

Flora MacTaggart
1812 - 1892

Jessie
b. 1845

Isabella
1840 - 1906

Alexander
1830 - 1836

Margaret
b. ca 1833 - 1895

Ann or Nancy
b. ca 1834 - 1877

Dugald**
1836 - 1877

Mary
1837 - 1925

m.

m.

m. 1869

m.

William Campbell

James Brandon
b. ca 1828

Helen Morison
1844 - 1872

Alexander Campbell
b. ca 1822 - d. bef. 1913

Isabella Campbell
1857 - 1925

m.

Robert J. Graham
1850 - 1928

\*    *illegitimate son with Ann Sinclair: James 1820 - 1871*
\*\*  *illegitimate daughter with Mary Clark: Grace b. 1868*

The earliest Johnstons are buried on the East side of the chapel on Kilnaughton Cemetry. In the old Gaelic tradition, people held in high esteem were buried on the east side outside a chapel or church, based upon the belief that those buried on that spot would be the first to see the Lord at his Second Coming. Foreground: Gravestone of founder Donald Johnston. To the left, standing: John Johnston of Tallant.

Mr Alexr Johnston
Distiller Laphroaig

Glasgow 16 November
1836

Dear Brother

I do hereby offer, and you have agreed to accept of Three hundred and fifty pounds sterling. cash. or a bill at three months date including interest. as a full consideration and payment for your whole interest in the Laphroaig distillery Islay and its concerns. together with the whole stock of horses cattle farming utensils. household furniture now in the house at Laphroaig or upon the lands - or otherwise at grass - and in short for every thing pertaining to us in any way connected with the distillery and farm — Me taking upon me the payment of the entire of the debts of the concern. and freeing and relieving you of the same from and after this date — I also undertake in the event of your leaving the country / to exert myself to the utmost in collecting all the private accounts due to you for meal. and I shall use my best endeavour to get payment from the people in barley. for which I shall afterwards account to you at the current price of the country - and in the

mean

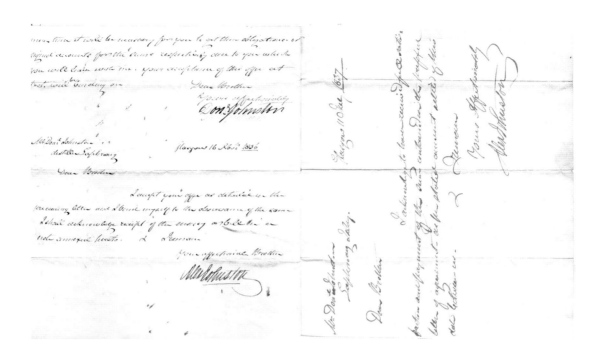

In 1835 Laphroaig was joined by another distillery at adjacent Ardenistle Farm (also spelled Arden-istiel or Ardinistle), financed by James and Andrew Gairdner and run by James and Andrew Stein, on a piece of land they leased from Campbell. Donald had fruitlessly protested against these plans a year earlier. He was afraid it might cause problems with the water supply to Laphroaig, as Ardenistle was only two hundred yards away. A letter from 1834 kept in the archives of Glasgow University, contains Donald's protests against a neighbouring distillery. A letter of agreement between Donald Johnston and James Stein survived, dated 1840. The agreement deals with exchanging land and water rights. Both distilleries would continue to have their quarrels – usually about that same topic of rights.

In 1836 Donald offered his brother Alexander £350 for his share, to which the latter agreed. In today's money that would be roughly £90,000. A year later the deal was struck and Donald became the sole owner of Laphroaig.

## Down Under

Alexander emigrated to Australia. He embarked on the 'Portland' and left Greenock on the 23rd of July 1837 to arrive in Australia the 3rd of December 1837. He had married his wife Flora MacTaggart that same year. Obviously his emigration was the reason for selling his share in Laphroaig. There were some 300 emigrants on board, many of them from Islay. It was a time when many Scots emigrated to Australia and Canada. The first mention of Islay whisky in Australia dates from 15 July 1839 when a few puncheons of the 'finest Islay whisky' were offered for sale in the *Sydney Monitor & Commercial Advertiser*.

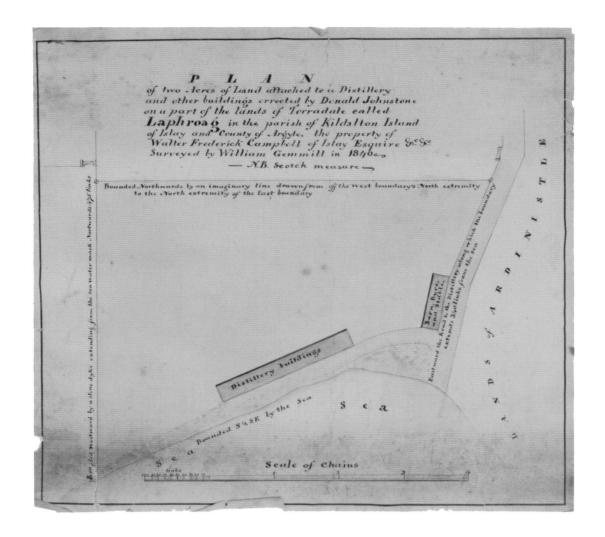

After initially being employed as a police officer, Alexander later found work on a farm in New South Wales, where his overseer was a J. Campbell from Islay. Apparently Campbells and Johnstons stick together, wherever they are in the world. Around 1853 Alexander managed to buy a tract of land in Moruya, New South Wales, and became an independent farmer, as he had been on Islay. Eventually Alexander died on 13 October 1881 and was buried in Sandgate Cemetery, Newcastle. He was survived by Flora and their nine children. When contacted, direct descendants of Alexander Johnston were thrilled with the fact that their Scottish ancestor's role in the history of Laphroaig was unveiled.

Originally the farm-distillery of Laphroaig consisted of two long narrow rectangular buildings, adjacent to one another. The west part was the distillery; the east part housed a barn, byre and stable. Plans from 1840 in the distillery archives illustrate this situation. They also mention a pond (or dam) on annexed land slightly to the north.

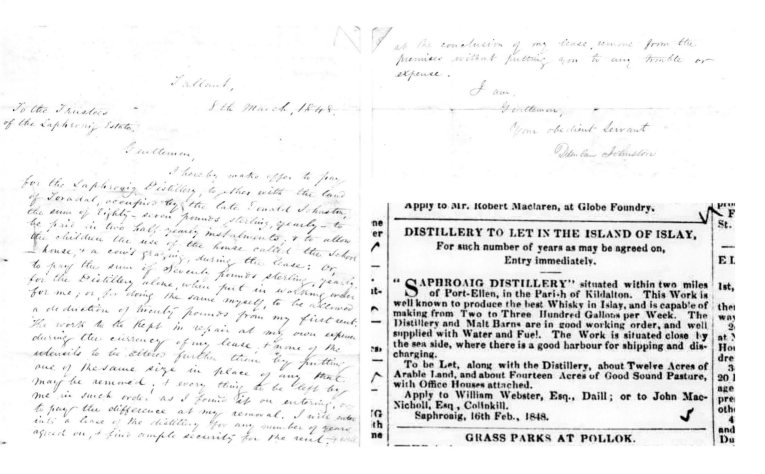

Sallant,

To the Trustees                 8th March, 1848.
of the Laphroaig Estate.

    Gentlemen,

             I hereby make offer to pay
for the Laphroaig Distillery, together with the land
of Toradal, occupied by the late Donald Johnston,
the sum of Eighty-seven pounds sterling, yearly - to
be paid in two half yearly instalments; & to allow
the children the use of the house called the School
house, & a cow's grazing, during the lease: Or,
to pay the sum of Seventy pounds sterling, yearly,
for the Distillery alone, when put in working order
for me; or, for doing the same myself, to be allowed
a deduction of twenty pounds from my first rent.
The work to be kept in repair at my own expense
during the currency of my lease, & none of the
utensils to be altered further than by putting
one of the same size in place of any that
may be removed, & every thing to be left by
me in such order as I found it on entering, or
to pay the difference at my removal. I will enter
into a lease of the distillery for any number of years
agreed on, & find ample security for the rent. & will

at the conclusion of my lease, remove from the
premises without putting you to any trouble or
expense.

            I am,
            Gentlemen,
            Your obedient Servant
            Duncan Johnston

Laphroaig whisky was soon exported to the USA. An 1846 ad in the *New York Morning Courier* read: 'Malt Whiskey-Ardbeg, Islay and Campleton, received direct from the distiller-Also, (for mixing) one puncheon of the celebrated Laphroig, for sale by CLEMENT D. MARCH (late Schermerhorn & March) no.26 Beaver st.'

## The Trust

Donald Johnston did not live to see the next apparent growth as shown on plans fourteen years later. It is generally believed that he died in June 1847 after having fallen in a vat of his own burnt ale, a residue from the pot stills. Donald's son Dugald more or less inherited the distillery but couldn't run it immediately. He was only eleven at the time. Donald had also fathered an illegitimate son named James, with a certain Ann Sinclair. We know this because at the time it was perfectly normal to write 'Illegitimate' on birth certificates. This humiliating practise was finally outlawed in 1919. Bastards did not count, and as census information from that period showed, James was supposedly deaf and dumb. (The census at the time offered the following additional categories: 1) deaf and dumb 2) blind 3) imbecile or idiot 4) lunatic). So the heir was Dugald.

The young heir's uncle John Johnston of Tallant acted as Trustee for his nephew, together with a local farmer called Peter MacIntyre. The former took great care of Laphroaig. On 3 March 1848, the curators of the ruined Walter Frederick Campbell offered Saphroaig [sic] for rent in the *Glasgow Herald*. Duncan Johnston from Tallant responded with a letter dated 8 March the same year, with a proposal to lease the distillery. The next day the experienced Lagavulin distiller Walter Graham put in his bid and was rewarded the lease of the property. It remains an interesting question why Duncan, almost certainly related to the Johnstons of Laphroaig, was passed over.

The other neighbour, Ardenistle also known at times as Ardenistiel, Islay or Kildalton Distillery, led a rocky life. The Stein brothers, belonging to a noted distilling family in Clackmannanshire and closely related to John Ramsay, adequately led the distillery from 1835 till 1846, when Andrew died and James subsequently moved to Port Ellen distillery. Andrew and James Gairdner, who held the original lease of the land of Ardenistle and had financed the distillery, offered the distillery to 'let or sell' in the *Glasgow Herald* on 7 February 1845. Apparently another kinsman of John Ramsay, a certain John Morrison, responded. Morrison had been wreaking havoc since 1826 at Port Ellen distillery and its Glasgow agency in various functions, but it seems the Gairdners gave him the benefit of the doubt.

In 1847 the lease of Ardenistle distillery was assigned to John Morrison but it did not work out. Within one year he failed again and the Excise Office eventually withdrew his license in 1851. He went bankrupt in 1852 and departed Islay for Glasgow as an embittered man. William Hunter and John Ferguson Sharpe took over the lease in 1851, but they couldn't do much about it and finally assigned lock, stock and barrel to Robert Salmond of the City and Glasgow Bank. Of course this was not to the amusement of Kildalton-laird John Ramsay. However he decided to renew the Ardenistle lease once more in 1859, this time to William and Andrew Hunter, for 19 years.

It would be a battle against time. In the mid 1860s William Hunter threw in the towel after never having reached full production. John Ramsay subsequently decided to close the distillery and brought Ardenistle under the Johnstons of Laphroaig, who found other use for the buildings in the form of an expansion to their own distillery.

## Meanwhile at Laphroaig

Uncle John Johnston had managed to renew the lease for the farm and distillery with the new laird James Morrison in 1854. Walter Graham who now acted as manager did well too, as plans from that same year show. The distillery building was enlarged at the west side and at the east side an L-shaped structure appeared, 'distilling house' later referred to as 'managers house' or 'Laphroaig House'. Graham also claimed to have 'nearly doubled the capabilities of Laphroaig Distillery since 1848'. He lived in Ardenistle House and leased the eponymous farm. The map right, drawn in 1854 for a new lease, shows the stables converted into an L- shaped 'distilling house', which would later become the foundation of Laphroaig House.

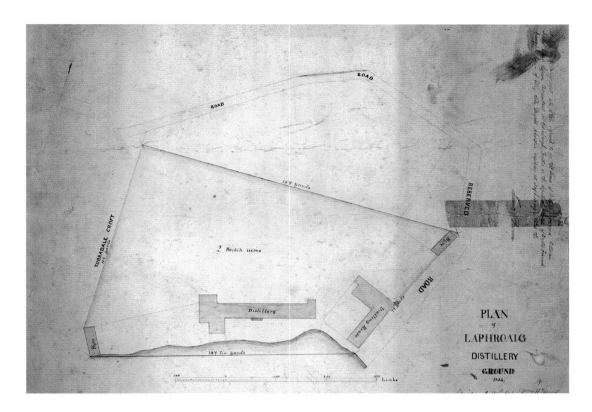

In 1857 Dugald came of age, took over the management and was assigned the land lease by his father's Trustees in 1858 in a new lease with Laird John Ramsay. The distillery-owner faced troubled times. His sisters Mary, Isabella, Margaret and Ann or Nancy disputed the assignment of Laphroaig to their brother. Apart from that he was confronted with more deadly accidents at the distillery. *The Stirling Observer* recorded on 26 January 1860: 'Angus Campbell, one of the workmen at Laphroag Distillery, Ilsley, went down to clear one of the tuns; he was rendered insensible by an accumulation of carbonic acid gas remaining in the tun. Another of the workmen, named M'Duffy ventured down to render assistance, when he also became insensible. Campbell was found to be quite dead. M'Duffy has recovered.' Various other newspapers recorded that at least four deadly accidents at Laphroaig had occurred before 1860. Health and safety regulations were a vague notion in those days.

Furthermore Walter Graham hadn't secured the water rights exclusively for Laphroaig to the Surnaig burn (as the source was called before Kilbride Reservoir was created). It supplied Ardenistle distillery, as registered in the lease of that property. This had been a sensitive point with Donald Johnston so it was understandable that Dugald became angry about this 'neglect'.

He withdrew sales of Laphroaig from the Islay Cellar in Glasgow, then owned by the Grahams. That didn't go down well with them. Then Dugald had to deal with Laird John Ramsay, who wasn't happy at all with the poor performance of Ardenistle Distillery and Farm. In the late 1860s he decided to join Ardenistle with Laphroaig, and Ardenistle as a distillery ceased to exist.

Finally Dugald solely owned the highly desired exclusive water rights to the Surnaig burn. Luckily he also got help from another member of the very clannish Johnston family: his cousin Alexander 'Sandy' Johnston from the Tallant branch. Sandy happened to be Dugald's brother-in-law through marriage to Dugald's youngest sister Isabella. (Check out the family tree on pages 34-35 again, if you have, understandably, lost track.) Dugald and Sandy ran the distillery side by side until the former died on 6 January 1877.

Dugald Johnston is portrayed as the founder of Laphroaig Distillery, as can be seen on the picture right. Historically this is incorrect since his father Donald officially registered Laphroaig in 1826. However the 'D' in the company name D. Johnston & Co. stands for Dugald, as can be read in legal documents. It is safe to assume that Donald also used 'Laphroaig' as the company name. Dugald was married to Helen Morison, but apparently they were not blessed with children. He did have an illegitimate daughter named Grace, fathered with a servant girl by the name of Mary Clark. She was certainly not in line to inherit the distillery.

## Sandy's Reign

The legal dispute over the assignment of the distillery still ran, which resulted in appointing three people as Trustees of the late Dugald Johnston's estate: Colin Hay of Ardbeg, James Logan Mackie and John Crawford Graham, the latter being Walter's brother. The Mackies played an important role as agents for Laphroaig. Thanks to them, Laphroaig appeared in Australia in 1880, advertised as part of a brand called Staghound, a 6-year-old vatted malt, consisting of Lagavulin and Laphroaig. At the time the Mackie's owned the former and acted as agent for the latter distillery.

Laphroaig distillery is mentioned specifically on 8 February 1881 when J.J. Burns office in Brisbane again announced the availability of Staghound Brand in Queensland, 'The Islay Blend Whisky, Mackie & Co, Lagavulin and Laphroaig Distilleries, Island of Islay, Staghound Brand, 6 years old'. It also described Laphroaig as the smallest of the Islay distilleries situated 'by the margin of the sea' and 'considered by connoisseurs to be inferior to none'. The Mackies would cause a lot of trouble for Laphroaig later on.

The three Trustees functioned together for a decade, during which period Sandy Johnston acted as distillery manager. In 1887 the Trustees decided not to renew the existing lease, which offered laird John Ramsay the opportunity to renegotiate with the Johnstons. Dugald's sister Isabella took the new lease, together with her husband Sandy, her sister Mary and Isabella, Mary's daughter.

The new lease, that would expire in 1905, not only covered the distillery but also water rights to the Surnaig burn, peat cutting rights in its adjacent fields, Laphroaig farm, Texa Island, Torradale Park and all buildings belonging to the former Ardenistle Distillery, which included 'the Bonded Warehouse and Dwelling House which belonged to Ardenistle Distillery and the Dwelling House presently occupied by John Douglas, Officer of Inland Revenue…'

DUGALD JOHNSTON

Founder of Laphroaig Distillery

Given by his great niece Molly Graham

Sandy Johnston had already started a big renovation plan in 1884, expanding some existing buildings and adding new ones. A photograph taken around this time shows the extensions to Laphroaig, as well as the ruins of Ardenistle farm and distillery. First Laphroaig House was rebuilt and a new byre was added, new stables followed in 1888 and Warehouse No.3 in 1889.

As can be seen in the picture of 1886 (on page 48), the year Alfred Barnard visited Laphroaig, the west end was an open structure; this building was probably used for cooling the wort before fermentation. The maltings are under construction (middle section of the image). Today's offices seem to be already present, using one of the described, surviving dwelling houses of Ardenistle. The little road along the shore would later be relocated north of the main building. The house in the back (right) is referred to as Bleak House, built around 1880. It originally served as the Excise Officer's house. The ruins in the right bottom corner would have been part of the remains of Ardenistle Distillery, now nicknamed 'Lavender Square'. Around 1900 the barn consisted of two storeys and the west end of the complex looked more consolidated. Another three warehouses (4, 5 and 6) were erected on the west side of the distillery grounds.

In 'How to Blend Scotch Whisky', published around 1900, chronicler Alfred Barnard writes: *'Laphroaig, notwithstanding a few necessary alterations to increase the output, still retains its venerable appearance, and its buildings exhibit specimens of curiously constructed places, so quaint that they would puzzle the understanding of an architect of the present day.'*

Now Sandy could prepare Laphroaig for the 20th century. He renewed the lease of the property in 1904 for another 15 years. A second Excise Officer's House was built around that time, called Tigh-an-arbhair. In 1905 he fell seriously ill. Sadly his wife died a year later on 18 June 1906, leaving him as her sole heir. It must have been a great blow to him since his younger sister Catherine, decided to move in with him from Tallant to assist him with his daily duties, as well as running the household. Sandy only survived his wife one year. On 17 June 1907 he died at Laphroaig.

Catherine, a down-to-earth woman, immediately seized power over the estate. However, Sandy's trustees found that he had left four wills. The first one was drawn in 1890 together with his now deceased wife Isabella Johnston. A second, third and fourth will were drawn by Sandy alone, on 28 January 1905, 16 February 1906 and 4 June 1906 respectively.

In his last will, Sandy named four heirs: his old friend and banker Duncan McKenzie, his sister Catherine, his nephew John Johnston Hunter Johnston and his niece by marriage Isabella Campbell (later to marry Robert J. Graham). When she found out, Catherine didn't particularly like the situation. It left out William S. Hunter, married to her sister Isabella, and favoured Isabella Campbell who was not directly related to Catherine.

A woman of great determination, Catherine convinced Duncan McKenzie and John Johnston Hunter Johnston to let her brother-in-law William S. Hunter join, based on the February 1906 will.

*Alexander 'Sandy' and Isabella Johnston*

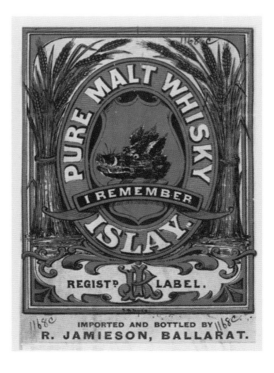

*1886*

*1900*

LAPHROAIG DISTILLERY, ISLAY.

*1904*

*circa 1910*

She then persuaded Sandy's law firm Menzies, Bruce-Low & Thomson of Edinburgh, to write a letter to laird Ramsay's factor Peter Reid, dated 12 August 1907 in which they stated that Catherine was the beneficiary of Sandy Johnston. Then the laird received a request to renew the lease with Catherine, her sister Isabella and their nephew John. Apparently Ramsay wanted to know what was going on and he asked for an explanation, which was given by Menzies et al. in a letter to Reid, dated 26 August 1907. It is a nice example of the way an early 20th century law firm tries to avoid being overly explicit.

## The Johnston-Hunters at the Helm

It took Ramsay some time to decide, but in the end it worked for Catherine since Ramsay granted a new lease to the threesome. The decision also meant that the Kildalton-branch of the Johnston family who started the distillery would no longer be involved. The late Sandy Johnston's excluded in-laws, Mary and her daughter Isabella, had already started legal action against Sandy taking a new lease without them in 1904. The court case dragged on past Sandy's death. This was to no avail since John Johnston Hunter Johnston, Catherine, Isabella and her husband William Stevenson Hunter (opposite page) eventually secured the lease in 1911 for twenty years. The Tallant branch had won and the Kildalton branch was silenced. It would take another 16 years before the last Johnston disappeared from the Laphroaig stage.

The Hunters had only one child, Ian William, who was immediately groomed by his parents to manage the distillery. Since neither his aunt Catherine nor his cousin John Johnston Hunter Johnston had descendants, he would eventually become the sole heir of the Tallant-Johnston branch of the family. Ian was sent to Glasgow for training as an engineer. Cousin John managed the distillery at the time. From 1908, when he returned to Islay, Ian Hunter played a more prominent role as manager of the distillery. In 1910 he probably wrote but definitely signed a detailed plan recording the existing layout of the distillery, before the impending alterations.

The Royal Commission on the Ancient and Historical Monuments of Scotland (RCAHMS) sought out the 1910 plan from the Laphroaig archives in 1980. In their survey (see also the map on page 53), handed to the distillery later that year, they described the situation in 1910 as follows: 'a model of working-efficiency for a small distillery of that time. It consists of a central mash-house flanked by a tun-room and still-house on either side, and there is also an integral spirit-store and draff-shed. The mash-house contains a mash-tun, underback and two heating-coppers, and also a Morton refrigerator, conveniently placed next to the tun-room and its five (sic) washbacks.

*1903*

*Ian Hunter with Calum McAffer on the pillion.*

The two stills are set against the north wall of the still-house and connect with two worm-tubs outside; the still-house also contains the wash-charger, chargers and receivers for the low-wines and feints, and the intermediate spirit-receiver, the latter being connected to the main receiver in the adjoining spirit-store. A steam engine operating at that time was evidently situated in the re-entrant angle between the still-house and the mash-house... The 1924 site plan, previously referred to, continues to show a two-still arrangement and up till that time there appears to have been a a water wheel probably driven from the overflow of the worm tubs...'

The 1910 plan helped Ian Hunter to start the expansions in a structured way. In 1913 the famous distillery architect Charles Doig presented him with a drawing for new offices. When his father died in 1919, Ian took over his place in the partnership with his aunts. Between 1921 and 1923 he purchased the distillery and farm grounds, Texa Island and Ardenistle House from laird Iain Ramsay. Now Hunter could invest in his own property, freed from a lease that had to be renewed every so many years. He re-sited the old service road along the shore to a stretch north of the malt barn, which was itself expanded in 1924 to its current height of three storeys.

Probably already in 1878, but definitely by 1924, the original warehouses 1 and 2 were joined together with the offices (formerly a dwelling house of Ardenistle). Warehouses were renumbered on various occasions over the years. The current warehouse No. 1 was built on the ruins of Ardenistle in 1924. First the west side was raised, consisting of two parallel buildings, each one story high. Later that year the east side was added, three storeys high. Thirteen years later, in 1937, the west side was raised to its present height of three storeys. The current warehouse No. 7 was erected in 1928.

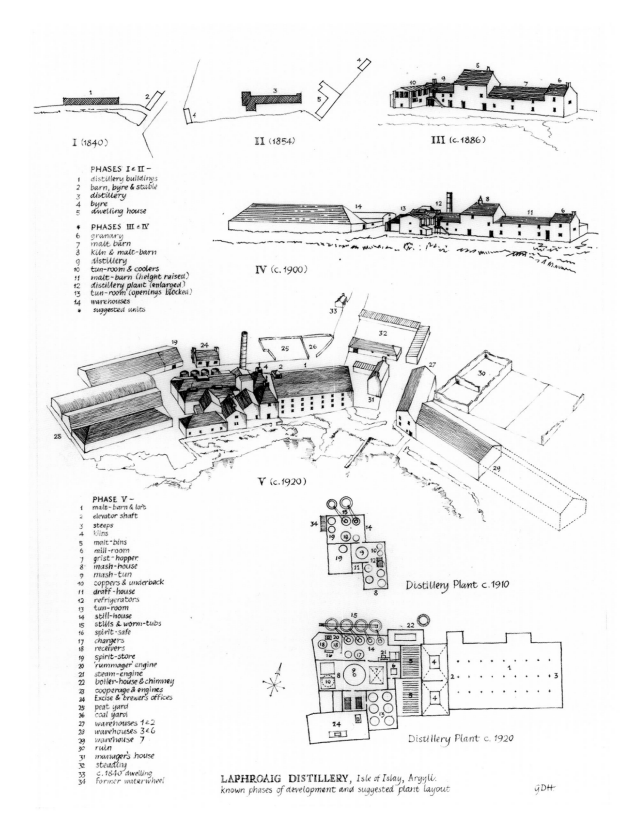

I (1840)

II (1854)

III (c.1886)

IV (c.1900)

PHASES I & II –
1 distillery buildings
2 barn, byre & stable
3 distillery
4 byre
5 dwelling house

* PHASES III & IV
6 granary
7 malt barn
8 kiln & malt-barn
9 distillery
10 tun-room & coolers
11 malt-barn (height raised)
12 distillery plant (enlarged)
13 tun-room (openings blocked)
14 warehouses
* suggested units

V (c.1920)

PHASE V –
1 malt-barn & loft
2 elevator shaft
3 steeps
4 kilns
5 malt-bins
6 mill-room
7 grist-hopper
8 mash-house
9 mash-tun
10 coppers & underback
11 draff-house
12 refrigerators
13 tun-room
14 still-house
15 stills & worm-tubs
16 spirit-safe
17 chargers
18 receivers
19 spirit-store
20 'rummager' engine
21 steam-engine
22 boiler-house & chimney
23 cooperage & engines
24 Excise & brewer's offices
25 peat yard
26 coal yard
27 warehouses 1 & 2
28 warehouses 3 & 6
29 warehouse 7
30 ruin
31 manager's house
32 steading
33 c. 1840 dwelling
34 former waterwheel

Distillery Plant c.1910

Distillery Plant c.1920

LAPHROAIG DISTILLERY, Isle of Islay, Argyll.
known phases of development and suggested plant layout

GDH.

Laphroaig, Islay. — 1925/1926

From 1924 onwards the still house and mash house were extended, the tun room enlarged to contain six wash backs and two Morton refrigerators, used for cooling the wort. A jetty was built in 1925.

Doubling the still capacity was the most radical change. Laphroaig now had two wash stills and two spirit stills. The former two were equipped with the usual rummagers and all four of them were direct coal-fired. A small block of offices was built at the far west end near then-warehouse No. 6 for the use of the Excise Officer as well as employees. Peat and coal yards were located north of the malt barn. Farming still took place, cattle being kept on the distillery premises.

## Steam

The waterwheel disappeared; a coal fired Wilson boiler and steam engines were purchased. The number of steam engines at Laphroaig appears to have varied through the years. Ian Hunter must have been fond of steam engines; a few scale models were displayed in his office on a long table. In the early 1920s there had been only two steam engines, a vertical Tangye and a horizontal Tangye. Electricity was installed - probably in 1925 - at first only used for lighting.

In 1926 Ian's aunt Catherine died at 80. When finally his mother Isabella died in 1927, aged 84, he became sole owner of the property and the Johnston name disappeared from the title (but not from the bottle!).

The whitewashed buildings of Laphroaig now framed the small bay. Two pagodas crowned the kilns and a round chimney pushed into the sky. Several small causeways were built into the bay to create easier access for loading and unloading the Clyde puffers – small steamboats that were used to carry supplies to and from the West Coast and the Hebrides. In earlier days smaller boats had to unload these ships in the bay and were drawn by horses to the shore.

## The Mackies

Ian Hunter not only expanded the capacity of the distillery but also planned an international market growth for Laphroaig whisky. For 70-80 years the Mackies of neighbouring Lagavulin had acted as agents for Laphroaig, to the satisfaction of Hunter's predecessors. However, the heirs of Sandy Johnston refused to renew the contract in 1908, advised by their lawyers Menzies, Bruce-Low & Thomson. They stated that Mackie performed poorly and suggested John Johnston Hunter Johnston take a contract with Stodart & Wilson. Their action led to a court case with Peter Mackie, a descendant from James Logan Mackie, once a Trustee of Dugald Johnston. Ever since the latter inherited the distillery from his father Donald, it seemed a normal part of Laphroaig's life to be entangled in legal battles.

At first Ian Hunter wanted to sell Laphroaig whisky directly to customers after having ended the agreement with Mackie in court. Soon he must have felt that wasn't the best of decisions and indeed signed an agreement with Stodart & Wilson, since that company was highly recommended to him by several business friends. Letters from the archives show that Hunter was already negotiating with the new agent before the contract with Mackie was ended. The new company briefly acted as agent but was soon followed by a company called Robertson & Baxter.

Peter Mackie was mad with rage at the loss of the agency and decided to do something very peculiar about it. He was going to make his own Laphroaig-style whisky. But before doing so he took Hunter to court and...lost. Using stones he blocked Laphroaig's water supply...and was ordered to re-open it. As a consequence, Hunter started to buy all the land above the distillery following the stream up to its source.

Mackie's rage was understandable, since his family had built Laphroaig's reputation as an excellent whisky. So, what do you do when you can't get Laphroaig anymore to sell to your customers? Build your own Laphroaig! At least that was Peter Mackie's answer to Ian Hunter's refusal to renew the contract with him as an agent for Laphroaig. Mackie already owned neighbouring Lagavulin Distillery and decided he would fiercely compete with Hunter.

In 1908 he lured Laphroaig's brewer away, built a still exactly the same size as Laphroaig's and started distilling. He called his new distillery-in-a-distillery Malt Mill. Sad but true for Mackie, he never succeeded in copying the unique flavour of his neighbour. Malt Mill was merged with Lagavulin in the early 1960s. Its coal-fired stills went to the Lagavulin still house and its former building is the current reception area at Lagavulin. Mackie's blend White Horse, introduced in 1890, survives. A tiny bottle of Malt Mill can still be seen in a locked glass case, in the visitor centre at Lagavulin.

## Laphroaig as Medicine

Ian Hunter wanted to be involved in every aspect of the distillery. He was meticulous about everything and very suspicious. No outsider was allowed onto the premises and details about the distilling process were guarded as if they were the crown jewels. He found it very important to properly train his staff. Often he would choose youngsters who had finished school at age fifteen. They could choose between working on the farm or in the cooperage. Hunter then taught them to malt, mash and distil. At age eighteen they frequently knew the whole process.

1930s

Hunter began to travel abroad and strengthen the ties with his customers worldwide. Legend has it that he managed to continue exporting Laphroaig to the USA during Prohibition (1920-1933), using a loophole in American law: whisky used for medicinal purposes was allowed during that wretched time. The iodine-like character of Laphroaig must have convinced the US Government. In 1927 Hunter came back upon his decision to use agents and terminated the agreement with Robertson & Baxter. From then on the whisky was sold directly from Laphroaig Distillery.

In 1928 Hunter created a unique blend, using Laphroaig as its backbone, blending his whisky with The Glenlivet, Glen Grant and Caledonian Grain whisky. It was named Islay Mist and launched in honour of the Laird of Islay House son's coming of age. Since the 1970s, the label features the seal of Islay, a heraldic device of the Lords of the Isles.

After the repeal of Prohibition, Hunter intensified his travels to the Caribbean and North America. Various newspapers in the US showed that Schenley New York Distillers

2-371

NO. 320120

# The United States of America

To All To Whom These PRESENTS Shall Come:

**This is to Certify** That by the records of the UNITED STATES PATENT OFFICE it appears that IAN WILLIAM HUNTER, doing business as D. JOHNSTON & COMPANY, of Port Ellen, Isle of Islay, Scotland,

did, on the 28th day of June, 1934 , duly file in said Office an application for REGISTRATION of a certain

## TRADE-MARK

shown in the drawing for the goods specified in the statement, copies of which drawing and statement are hereto annexed, and duly complied with the requirements of the law in such case made and provided, and with the regulations prescribed by the COMMISSIONER OF PATENTS.

And, upon due examination, it appearing that the said applicant is entitled to have said TRADE-MARK registered under the law, the said TRADE-MARK has been duly REGISTERED this day in the UNITED STATES PATENT OFFICE, to

Ian William Hunter, doing business as D. Johnston & Company, his heirs or assigns.

This certificate shall remain in force for TWENTY YEARS, unless sooner terminated by law.

In Testimony Whereof I have hereunto set my hand and caused the seal of the PATENT OFFICE to be affixed, at the city of Washington, this eighteenth day of December, in the year of our Lord one thousand nine hundred and thirty-four, and of the independence of the United States the one hundred and fifty-ninth.

*Conway P. Coe*

*Commissioner of Patents.*

ATTEST:

*H. S. Miller*

Law Examiner.

11—9384b

*1928*

*1950s*

heavily advertised Laphroaig. They would ultimately own the distillery for a time after having purchased Laphroaig in 1962 (then part of Seager Evans/Long John Distillers).

Hunter had always appointed managers, usually for a timespan of eighteen months among whom Malcolm MacAffer (1924), Andrew Shaw (1929). But now he could leave Laphroaig in the capable hands of a Ms. Elizabeth 'Bessie' Leitch Williamson, whom he had given a job as a temporary secretary in 1934. Although Hunter, a big lover of dogs, was known to be ill-tempered, Bessie got along with him and stayed. She can be seen in a picture taken that year with the entire working force, standing in front of the worm tubs.

Iain Ramsay appeared in this picture since Ian Hunter had remained very friendly with the Ramsay's after having purchased the distillery grounds and surrounding areas from Iain's father Captain Ramsay, in the early 1920s. In World War II Iain Junior served as a pilot for the RAF and was tragically killed on 30 April 1942, age 35. He was married to Freda Landen who wrote two standard works about Islay. They had two children, Janna and Eila. Eila has fond memories of Ian Hunter, who she remembers as 'rather shy', and of Bessie Williamson, as can be read in a memoir she wrote for us, reminiscing about a Christmas lunch at Callumkill in 1943:

*Standing (left to right): Jean Carmichael, Hugh McDougall, Hugh McLean, Iain McLean, Alister Logan, Alister McEachern, Malcolm Logan, Dougald Campbell, Ian W. Hunter (seated on barrel), Henry Urquhart, Pilot Officer Iain Ramsay, John Johnston, John McEachern, John Logan (on barrel), Allan Carmichael, Bella McDougall, Elizabeth L. Williamson (Bessie). Kneeling (left to right): James McColl, Angus McTaggart, Euan Gillies, Dugald Sinclair.*

*'My widowed mother Freda Ramsay invited Ian Hunter, friend of all my family for many years and his assistant Bessie Williamson, to join us all for Christmas lunch at Callum Kill House. They arrived by car carrying parcels. After dinner Ian Hunter and my grandfather sat in front of the fire trying to light the Christmas pudding with Islay Mist but it just didn't light. Ian was very cross. He got to his feet and telling Bessie to stay there with us, he left. He returned with a bottle in an old piece of brown paper and put it into my Mother's hand saying 'Freda THAT WILL BURN'. Later, long after my bedtime I could hear them all talking and laughing. The bottle that Ian had brought back, my Grandfather looked after because it was very dusty and did not have a label on it!'*

Hunter also made himself useful as a member of the Commission of the Peace, which he had joined in 1933, finding John Granville Morrison and Captain Iain Ramsay as co-members on the board. This organisation dealt with petty crime on the island and acted as a lay type of court. Around 1938 Hunter suffered a stroke while abroad and immediately arranged for Bessie to fly to the USA and attend the business meetings, negotiating in his place. During their absence, a certain A. Thomson was appointed as distillery manager. He came from Dufftown, where he had been brewer at Glenfiddich for some years.

*Around 1930*

## Wartime

World War II caused troubled times for most distillers in Scotland and production stopped altogether to save barley for food supplies. A few distilleries were excepted from the rule, but Laphroaig was not one of them. Instead the distillery was mothballed. The First Company of Royal Engineers was housed in the malt barns shortly after the Battle of Dunkirk (May-June 1940). Their task was to enlarge Glenegedale Airport and protect the western approaches. The barley loft at the malt barns was used as a cinema to show films to the troops. Laphroaig House was taken over for Royal Air Force personnel.

Distillery employees attended to the requirements of the RE and RAF men. Apart from not distilling, regular life went on as usual, such as warehouse work, peat cutting, farm work, maintenance of machinery and distillery equipment. Sales continued and even increased since Laphroaig was supplying the military's messes all over the UK. The 'occupation' didn't arouse much trouble, mainly small incidents regarding the men trying to help themselves to a dram. After the Servicemen departed in 1943/44, the malt barns were converted into ammunition stores.

Laphroaig was compensated for the requisitioning of their property. From 1943 on Hunter received an annual sum of £120 from the Ministry of Works for the usage of the distillery buildings. Employees were compensated for work they did in those years. A certain Ewan Gillies, for instance, received 19 shilling 6d for 18 hours of work. This would currently be worth about £40. Evidence of Laphroaig's usage during the war is not only from archives and memories. There is proof of that today: some warehouses still have blackout smudge on the upstairs windows.

On 23 March 1944, Ian Hunter informed the Ministry that he relinquished the management of the distillery to Bessie Williamson, due to health related problems. In August the same year the Ministry of Supplies announced that barley could be delivered again for distilling purposes. Early 1945, Laphroaig was up and running again. Hunter finished building a couple of cottages behind the distillery whose construction had started in 1939 but could not be completed during the war. In effect he was the first to get a permit to build after the war had ended. Hunter's physical condition unfortunately deteriorated and he became bound to a wheelchair, suffering from arteriosclerosis.

He approached several of his distant relatives and tried to interest them in taking over the distillery, but didn't succeed in persuading them and changed the legal form of the enterprise into a limited company in 1951. He granted Bessie Williamson a small portion of the shares.

*1940s*

*Left to right: Calum Logan, Bessie Williamson, Ian Hunter.*

*Ian Hunter taking samples in the office.*

## Rachel and Bessie

Laphroaig continued to grow and prosper until Ian Hunter died in 1954 at the age of 68. He left all employees with 10 years or more continuous service at Laphroaig the princely sum of £100. Rachel McAffer, who had joined the company in 1935 as a secretary, was rewarded even a ten-fold. Over time she had become the 'company walking archive'. She was even called upon to document facts 50 years later, after her retirement. In a 1988 letter addressed to Nick Redman, archivist at Whitbread - the then owner of Laphroaig - Rachel reported some interesting events, partly told to her by her then 85-year old brother Calum who worked for Ian Hunter, beginning in the 1920s. One of these anecdotes illustrates how meticulous Ian Hunter was regarding the quality of Laphroaig. When the public road to the distillery was reconstructed, Hunter discussed with the Argyll & Bute County Council what tar should be used. He wanted to be assured that the tar would not have any detrimental effect on the distillery water. At the time this water flowed in an open ditch to the distillery. According to Rachel McAffer, rubble from Lavender Square, originally a part of Ardenistle distillery, was used for the new road. So, in a way, visitors who today approach Laphroaig will walk over a piece of 'old Ardenistle'.

Rachel McAffer also reported the installation of the private telephone exchange in Laphroaig House, with connections to the distillery, the brewer's office, Bleak House, Ardenistle Cottage and Ardenistle House. When Hunter wanted to have public telephone installed on Islay he ran into an argument with the telephone company in    London. The general manager told Hunter that 'there was no need for telephones in such an outlandish Island'. Hunter didn't agree of course and telephone came to Islay, albeit a bit late.

Rachel McAffer must have been of great value to the company as a whole, but also to Ian Hunter in person. A special legacy in his will stated: 'To Rachel McAffer, £1000, for saving my life on two occasions'. One of these occasions happened to be a fire in the offices. Rachel reportedly dragged Ian Hunter, who had fallen unconscious out of the building.

Bessie Williamson received a legacy of £5000 and inherited the distillery, Ardenistle House and Texa Island. Thus she became the first woman in the 20th century to manage and own a Scottish whisky distillery. After his demise in 1954 Ian Hunter was still well remembered for improving and expanding Laphroaig. He had invested heavily in the distillery and on building the brand worldwide. At the time of his death he had recaptured once lost markets such as Scandinavia.

*1950s*

Scale model Tormore

Bessie in the USA

In the USA Laphroaig had firmly established its position as a premium single malt. In Scotland the whisky was much sought after by the blenders. In short, Bessie seemed to have inherited a flourishing business.

The Scotch Whisky Association immediately saw the unique selling point it would have when Bessie could be engaged in promoting Scotch whisky overseas. Soon she was lecturing on behalf of the SWA and other related organisations, travelling frequently to the USA using a scale model of sister distillery Tormore to explain distilling. She left the distillery in the hands of Tom Anderson, who had started working for Laphroaig in 1933, the same week that marked the arrival of Bessie on Islay. Anderson had made a nice career for himself, which had temporarily been broken off during the Second World War, when he was drafted. In 1945 he came back and commenced in the mash house and stillhouse, then working as a brewer. Though not officially appointed, he acted as manager as of 1954, the year his son Tom Jr. became boilerman at Laphroaig.

On one of her promotional trips Bessie met Mr Wishart Campbell, a famous singer. He was born on Islay but emigrated to Canada as a young boy. The couple fell in love and Campbell planned to move back to Scotland. On 15 August 1961 they were married in Glasgow, after which they moved to Ardenistle House. Local lore has it that Wishart Campbell arrived on the island with only two tangible assets: a suitcase and a white grand piano.

## Under American Ownership

Laphroaig whisky did well in sales. A new warehouse, number 8, was built in 1961. Farming ended at the beginning of 1963. However, the distillery was in dire need of repair. Bessie, now called Mrs Wishart Campbell, didn't have the resources to finance a thorough renovation, partly caused by the high death duties she had to pay as a result of inheriting the distillery. Being a smart businesswoman she approached the American Seager Evans drinks company, ultimately owned

*Bessie with Tom Anderson Sr.*

by Schenley Corporation, in 1962 and offered 33% of her shares for sale to its subsidiary Long John Distillers, who also owned Tormore Distillery in Speyside, among other ones. At the time Laphroaig employed 38 people.

The stills were remarkably smaller than today. In 1962 their capacities were: number 1 wash still 1,800 gallons, number 2 wash still 1,532 gallons, number 1 spirit still 753 gallons and number 2 spirit still 800 gallons. There were three steam engines, two Tangye and a Marshall; also two steam Weirs pumps. The big Tangye engine drove the water pump to fill the heating tanks, the worts pump, wash pump, the Boby mill and mash tun stirrer. If need be it could drive all the machinery in the malt barn. The small Tangye was situated below the spirit safe. It drove the low wines and feints pump and the rummagers in the wash stills.

In a letter to Long John that same year, Bessie sums up the assets: 'farm 471 acres including Ardenistle, Texa, Torradale. Houses: ten semi-detached cottages, one cottage [Ardenistle], Laphroaig House, Bleak House, two cottages currently being built on our ground. About the

personnel employed she writes: 'I agree about the pruning-but remember some of the older men have been here for many years and I have kept them on meantime as we have no pension scheme.' Farming at the distillery ended at the beginning of 1963.

Long John announced plans for the expansion of Laphroaig. On 9 May 1965, the *Sunday Times* recorded some of the modifications that lay ahead: 'The modernization – including new stills and more mechanical handling plant – will take Laphroaig's annual production from 200,000 gallons to 300,000 by the 1966-67 distilling season'. In 1967 Long John bought a second chunk of shares from Bessie and sent in a new manager by the name of Bill Scott. He replaced Tom Anderson who then became head brewer. Bill Scott's directive from Bessie was to ensure 'continuity of production'. He remained until 1970 when he went to Invergordon. When recently interviewed, Scott recalled some interesting production facts from the late 1960s:

Production was seven days a week at the time. The brewers yeast would arrive in casks on puffers from Glasgow. The main barley used was Golden Promise, which, according to Scott, had a low alcohol yield. In 1967 too much malted barley was produced on-site. In Scott's view this was to keep the old boys working towards or into retirement. The amount of peated malt onsite was reduced by Scott himself. The peat used at Laphroaig for malting was handcut, lower level/deep cut peat even though there were peat cutters who bought machinery and began cutting that way for the distillers. Fermentation would have been a minimum of 48 hours, or left longer to get as much alcohol as possible. Ex-bourbon as well as ex-sherry casks were in use. 'The wood was heavily impregnated with sherry'. Laphroaig in sherry wood was Scott's personal preference because it 'mellowed the smoke.' Scott seems to remember the casks were filled around 70% ABV, but was not entirely sure of that. The current manager's house, in front of the distillery, was built for Scott in 1969.

## Fire

In 1968 a fire broke out in the malt storage area. Laphroaig could not produce for six weeks because the mash tun had to be replaced. The original cast iron mash tun was replaced by a stainless steel one with a wedge wire floor. Other people involved remember that fire. Bill Rankin, at the time Supervising Engineer for Long John, recalled what happened: 'I remember the fire in the sixties. Bessie Williamson was still there. She was a fine person. On the morning after the fire we got a telephone call in Glasgow from Bessie telling us of the fire and it was decided we should go over. We chartered a plane and Bill Brown, Victor Thomson and I went across getting a good look at the scene on the way. The pilot circled the distillery for us. With temporary conveyors, production was not off for long. Fillings contracts were not upset! The cause of the fire, in my opinion at the time, was accumulation of malt dust which will auto ignite if damp and in sufficient quantity. The fire was in an elevator head where an accumulation of malt dust had self-ignited. This made it impossible to get malt to the mill or onwards. I do not recall much damage to the kilns but I think we operated on one kiln for a while.'

Bill Rankin started working at Schenley, parent company of Long John, in 1956 and would end his contract in 1982 to become Managing Director of Newmill Engineering in Elgin. His involvement with Laphroaig continued. He supplied the distillery with a new lauter mash tun in 1985. But let us return to the end of the 1960s.

The renovation plan commenced almost immediately, now that Long John held the majority of the shares in Laphroaig. The steam engines were removed. One Tangye was given to the Heriot Watt University in Edinburgh, another to the Scottish Society for the Preservation of Historical Machinery (SSPHM) and yet another lingers on in bits and pieces at the distillery.

*1960s*

*A condenser installled in 1967.*

In 1967 the old still house was decommissioned for distilling. Oil was cheap and the switch from coal to oil made economic sense. Because coal would no longer be used for production, the old coal and peat shed opposite the old still house became available for the stills. The new still house now contained five stills: two of the old spirit stills, a third new spirit still and two brand new wash stills, albeit positioned in reverse order compared to the old situation.

The old direct-fired spirit stills had to be fitted with new steam coils (see pages 70-71). The new wash stills had steam pans. The old still house was converted into a new boiler house. The Cornish coal fired boiler was replaced with a new Lancashire oil fired one. The former had been used mainly to supply steam for heating the water for mashing and was not sufficient for heating the new stills. Modern shell-and-tube condensers replaced the old worm tubs and were situated outside the still house. For refurbishment of the old shed, the walls were modified, part of one being replaced by a large perspex pane with the roof extended accordingly.

Boilers had been replaced in 1924 and 1955 too, which had proven to be a painstaking task. Early in the 20th century a new boiler would be transported from a ship into a small boat that was tugged into Laphroaig Bay. In 1967 there was still no roll-on roll-off ferry service. The only way to get a boiler in was to hire two barges, one for the boiler and one for a crane. Laphroaig had to call in the help of the army to get the 17-ton boiler to the distillery. A press release mentions:

*The transport problem was solved: loading the boiler on an Army Landing Craft at Rhu for an overnight journey to Islay 29th/30th May. Mr W.D. Rankin, Engineering Director of Long John Distillers organised the shipment and travelled on the landing craft. A safe landfall was made at 4 a.m. The supervising pilot was a man named...John Campbell.*

By the end of the decade quite some renovation had taken place but Long John still wasn't satisfied with the output of the distillery. The company clearly wanted more control over Laphroaig and moved one of its employees, John McDougall (right) - a self-proclaimed troubleshooter - from their Speyside distillery Tormore to Islay in 1970. He would face a formidable woman.

## Mrs Elizabeth 'Bessie' Leitch Williamson Campbell

Bessie's reputation was legendary. She was born on 22 August 1910 in Glasgow. Her father served with the Royal Garrison Artillery and was killed in action at the end of World War I in 1918. Bessie was raised by her mother, together with an older sister and younger brother. In 1927 she matriculated at the University of Glasgow. In 1932 she graduated and planned to become a teacher. While waiting for a vacancy she started working at her uncle William Paton's accounting firm and combined that job with attending night classes at the Glasgow and West of Scotland Commercial College.

In 1934 she saw and responded to an advertisement for shorthand typist at…Laphroaig Distillery. She got the position and prepared to stay on the island for three months. It would turn out to be a lifetime. Ian Hunter was duly impressed by her work and personality and came to trust her completely over the years. She won several prizes and was elected Woman of the Year in Great Britain in the 1950s. After her marriage to musician Mr. Wishart Campbell on 15 August 1961 in Glasgow Cathedral, she gradually relinquished control of the distillery. Bessie continued to live with her husband at Ardenistle House, tending her flowers and greenhouse, as well as organising musical and social events. Many of them she instigated for local charity and Bessie could always be called upon when someone dearly needed a job. For her charity work she was awarded the Order of St John. On occasion she even supplemented the wages of employees when they had drunk it all on payday. She also had the custom of employing men beyond retirement age because there was no pension scheme. An attitude like that creates a large following but isn't always healthy for the business.

Bessie's immense popularity among the Ileachs didn't make McDougall's task any easier, since he had to resort to unpopular measures such a firing redundant employees, making production more 'lean and mean' and stopping the habit of dramming. Before the mid 1970s dramming was a populair habit at many distilleries. At the start of their daily tasks the workforce would be offered a wee dram, to be followed by a couple more during the day. When an especially dirty job had to be done, an extra 'dirty' dram was given to the one who handled the job. It was not uncommon in earlier days to receive 5-8 drams during one working day. We are talking about new make spirit, not matured whisky!

Apart from all that, McDougall was an outsider, not born on Islay. It must not have been an easy period for the distillery, now mostly owned by an international drinks company. Bessie had to accept a second captain on the ship, a situation that would last until 1972 when she sold her last shares to Long John International and retired at Ardenistle House. Laphroaig now was no longer (partly) a privately owned company, but 100% part of an international conglomerate. A major change that would eventually benefit the company and its employees.

Bessie died on 26 May 1982, aged 71 at Gartnavel General Hospital in Glasgow. A few days before her demise she had joked to her niece Helen Powell: 'The first time I went to Islay was in a very small plane and the last time I go back to the mainland it will be a small plane' (the ambulance plane).

Her husband died one year later in 1983. Helen Powell recalls fond memories of her aunt in an email to us. It is a first-hand account of how Bessie Williamson was respected and loved.

> 'Aunt Bess left a will, Wish got the house and land including Texa island. Aunty Peggy was left all personal possessions and I was left the jewellery and money. Aunty Peggy did not want very much so I collected up a lot of memorabilia.

> Unfortunately from the time the will was made to the time Bess died, the money had gone and quite a sum was owed to the bank, so the house had to be sold and Wish moved into the White Hart Hotel where he remained until he became ill. He died in Bowmore Hospital in Nov 1983. Wish left me 1/3 of the residue, and 2/3 went to Canada for a nephew.

> I have lovely memories of a very lively Aunt who used to come to visit when I was a child and she would dance around the room with me.  Life was fun when we stayed at Ardenistle with large family and friends, picnics to the beach and parties at the house.

> Bess was very much part of the community, Ardenistle had a cook and housekeeper for many years so Bess had plenty of time to be involved. When she married of course she was very much missed by us all as she had a husband to look after. Wish had been in showbusiness all his life and was a good host. He was kind to us when we visited and as long as it was on his terms, good company!

> Ardenistle Nurseries was set up to give Wish a hobby, provide more local employment and help with taxes on Bess's salary. The gardens were always well kept and the estate managed. All this I assume cost a lot of money and eventually became a drain on resources once Bess retired from managing the distillery. Bess would never leave Ardenistle and as things worked out she did not have to. We visited the Summer before she died and took her over Jura for the day with our children. It was a lovely time.'

During the reign of Long John International, ultimately owned by the American Schenley Company, many modifications were made to modernise the distillery in order to produce more efficiently with a greater output. Warehouses number 3, 4, 5 and 6 were gradually pulled down. Laphroaig House, the old home of Ian Hunter, was demolished in 1972. Two American engineers were sent to Laphroaig to assess whether Schenley should keep or sell the distillery. It was for keeps. They came up with a number of improvements to be implemented by McDougall and his staff.

*1970s*

*1976*

Long John's Speyside distilleries showed a much greater yield than Laphroaig. McDougall introduced better cleaning procedures in fermentation, which directly influenced the yield of alcohol in a positive way. He managed to increase that yield from 2.54 proof gpb to 2.75 but that was still below a distillery like Tormore. It had to be explained to the Americans that the high peat level of Laphroaig was one of the reasons for the difference in output. To stop using the typical low sulphur peat known at Laphroaig meant that the whisky would lose its characteristic smokiness. That was not an option. Instead, the production capacity of Laphroaig was to be dramatically increased.

Many improvements would follow, such as installing a new fire ring main system. Not all upgrades were initially successful. The use of seawater in the condensers did increase the supply of process water (enough water available always having been a problem for Laphroaig), but it eroded the copper piping inside. This led to building a cooling tower and a dam behind the still house. Now the water from the still house condensers could be recycled and reused with fresh

*1976*

water. To regulate the flow of water even better, a new dam was built at Kilbride with which a reservoir could be created, capable of holding maximally five million gallons of water. Changing something at the source invariably causes consequences further down stream. Virtually every part of the distillery got its share of renovation. The maltings were updated by installing oil-fired burners in the kilns. As a result five or six batches of barley a week were malted, instead of the previous three runs, because the drying time was reduced from 48 to 30 hours. The tun room had to be expanded and three Corten steel wash backs were installed in 1976, in addition to the six Oregon pine wooden wash backs that had served Laphroaig for over 40 years, some even patched with cement.

The Isle of Islay frequently endured electrical power failures due to heavy gales and storms. Ships could not reach the island and distilleries had to temporarily stop production. Something that even happens today. To make Laphroaig less dependent on the whims of the weather it was decided by Long John to install a power generator on-site in 1971.

*1976*

## The Big Still

The still house had some minor alterations, which enabled a third wash still and a fourth spirit still being installed in 1972, increasing the total number of stills to seven. The added spirit still (the current Nr. 1) was twice the size of the existing three spirit stills and initially caused a lot of unrest with McDougall and his team. They preferred two additional spirit stills of the same size as they were used to, emphasising the point that the taste of Laphroaig would change using a different size of still. However, Long John insisted on the least expensive option and up till today the still house contains three wash stills and four spirit stills, of which one is notably bigger than the other three. It is said that the taste indeed changed, albeit slightly. The output of the four stills is mixed together, so any difference, should there be, will be evened out before maturation.

More spirit meant a larger cask-filling store, for which an old farm building was renovated into a new vat room. The old wooden spirit receiver replaced by a larger stainless steel one. The area

*1976*

where empty casks were taken in had to be enlarged. It created an opportunity to get rid of a lot of rubble and ruins. Small stables were torn down. New warehouses were also gradually built on the north side of the property next to the Kildalton Road. Ian Hunter, the last descendant of Laphroaig's founders Donald and Alexander Johnston who'd run and own the distillery, would not have recognised the place anymore.

Long John had definitely made its mark on Laphroaig, but ultimate owner Schenley only enjoyed the fruits of the renovation for a short time. In 1975 the American ownership ended when Seager Evans' subsidiary Long John International was taken over by the brewing company Whitbread, bringing Laphroaig back into British hands. Early in 1974 John McDougall had received company orders to swap places with Tormore-manager Denis Nicol, who then became the last distillery manager of Laphroaig under American and the first under renewed British ownership.

*Kneeling (left to right): Malcolm McEwan, John Cameron, P.J. MacCuaig, John Jagger, David Rice, Peter Paterson, Duncan Livingstone, William Livingstone.*
*Standing (left to right): Norman Campbell, Jimmy McCallum, Islay Livingstone, John Johnstone, David Livingstone, John MacNeill, David Adams, Denis Nicol, Donald Campbell, Peter MacGregor, Iain McLean, James McGregor, John MacNeill, Rachel McAffer, George Ingram, Alex Gunn, James Campbell, Betty MacAffer, Ian MacArthur, Morag Smith, Catherine Paterson, Archie McLellan, Mrs. Swarbrick, Gilbert MacCalman, Agnes Heads, Sid Bowman, Peter MacCuaig, Hector MacLean, Gordon McKechnie, James McFarlace, John Calder, Harry Newman, Dick Swarbrick.*

## Denis Nicol

John McDougall and Denis Nicol would stay colleagues after the takeover by Whitbread - who kept the name Long John alive - albeit both with a totally different challenge. McDougall could set his teeth in renovating Tormore, whereas Nicol found himself in a Laphroaig ready for increased production levels. That didn't mean it was an all-young crew. On the occasion of long-time employee Iain McLean's retirement in 1977 a picture was taken. Denis Nicol is standing to the left of McLean, with tie. Thanks to Eddie Morris, retired warehouseman, we were able to name all people in the picture.

Iain McLean was a remarkable employee and had worked in the Laphroaig warehouses most of his life. During World War II he was enlisted as a gunner in the 414 Battery, 146 Regiment, R.A., B.L.A. Immediately after the war a request from Laphroaig was sent to Col. D.W. Scott, Ministry of Food in Glasgow to release McLean as soon as possible because he was needed at Laphroaig. The letter explained the urgency of the matter, 'Vacancy advised to local Employment Exchange. No suitable man available. Advertised for cooper-warehouse in papers, several times. No suitable applicants.' In 1977 he was invited to London to receive a long-service award together with Rachel McAffer, Iain Hunter's former secretary.

Laphroaig apparently continued to stabilise its position worldwide. During Denis' reign the ancient Boby mill was replaced with a Porteus one. A chimney for the draff dryer was erected around 1975. During the 70s and 80s there was a lot of experimenting in distilling, results of which were not always understood.

Whitbread introduced Quality Assurance Management company-wide and appointed McDougall managing director of that department. Nicol, a scientist at heart, conducted gas chromatographic tests on Islay whiskies. He reported that 'the smells were remarkable. I sniffed peaks of aroma coming off the whisky. Apart from smells you would expect, like heather and sphagnum moss, there was peppermint that came from the bog myrtle, a plant that grows in boggy conditions. There was also the smell of yellow flag, a plant that has phenolic notes when the root is broken.'

## Murdo Reed

In 1980 Nicol, eventually being more interested in chemistry than in running a distillery, left Laphroaig to become a project scientist with Long John's laboratory. He was succeeded by Murdo Reed, who had started his career in the whisky industry at the age of 16, at Ardmore Distillery in Aberdeenshire. Murdo Reed arrived on Islay 4 August 1980 and found a distillery that direly needed renovation. Apart from the maltings, almost everything at Laphroaig needed to be changed. The new boiler house was started in 1980. The old one was a tip and the boiler was inefficient.

*1970s*

*1982*

*1985*

86

*Standing (left to right): Alistair Livingstone, Peter Campbell, Sammy Graham, Alan Hyslop, Michael Heads, Jim Kinloch, Duncan McIntyre, Michael Corson.*
*Seated (left to right): Arthur Holyoake, William Leask, Jim Baggley, Murdo Reed, Andrew Campbell, Colin Campbell, Duncan Livingstone.*

Production levels were low because of a dip in the industry. That made it possible to rebuild the still house in 1982 without a loss of production. Various publications mention, confusingly, that the still house was reversed. In fact the stills and condensers remained where they were, but the old wooden receivers were replaced by steel receivers and moved to the back. A big cast iron receiver served temporarily as wash charger and stood in front of the still house under construction. Originally the receivers would have been where the huge glass windows now are. It was, in Reed's words 'like a shanty town at the back of the still house, all plastic and glass'. Before reconstruction the condensers were located outside the still house. The new peat shed went in when the still house project was nearly finished. New malt bins were put in, which created space for a larger tun room. In May 1981 the old red brick chimney was torn down. The entire site temporarily resembled a building pit.

The mash and tun room was completely redone in 1985 and logic and temperature controllers were added. They automated the heat during fermentation instead of having operators control it. Six brand new stainless steel wash backs were installed. The three Corten steel washbacks were hard to clean and the six wooden ones were not efficient, hard to maintain and unhygienic. Stainless steel would give a more consistent production. This meant the definitive end of the wooden washbacks at Laphroaig. Due to this huge refurbishment, production came to a halt for five months.

Over some of the alterations heated discussions were held. Reed's boss at the time, Bill Rankin, wanted a stainless steel condenser on the wash still. Seawater was briefly considered for cooling in stainless condensers, but that was quickly scrapped. Reed was worried about the loss of copper contact in the condenser, but Rankin overruled him. However, the spirit was taking forever to clear from the foreshots. They couldn't get it to clear and Murdo described it 'a disaster'. He managed to continue production but it took until the next silent season to replace the stainless steel with copper.

A Cockayne automated cask filling system was introduced. This took the spirit receiver charge and pumped it through a metering system that corrected for density and temperature. Laphroaig could now actually measure how much went into a cask in bulk litres and litres of alcohol and assign it directly to the cask number. All was printed out, which was a big improvement for the administrative department. A change was made from brewers yeast to Mauri and DCL yeast. The main reason being 'for logistical purposes'. In 1987 he regrettingly had to decide for family reasons to leave Islay and moved on via Tormore and Glenmorangie to Invergordon Distillers in Tain, where he worked until his retirement.

In the seven years Murdo Reed managed the distillery, essential parts of the process were automated and the distillery was made ready to meet the next decade.

*1980s*

## Colin Ross

The next distillery manager was Colin Ross, who came from Tormore where he had worked with John McDougall. In 1977 he had already been on Islay to view Laphroaig, invited by Denis Nicol, who had been his boss at Tormore previously. About the same time Ross visited Glenugie, which obviously needed investment; it was clear to him that Long John had decided to invest in Laphroaig, not Glenugie. The latter would be closed for good in 1983 and Laphroaig was chosen for investment.

Upon his return to Islay a decade later, Ross could now make a good comparison between the old Laphroaig and the newly streamlined version for which Murdo Reed had been responsible. He arrived during the summer shutdown in August 1987. Ben Nevis Distillery, also owned by Whitbread at the time, had closed in 1986 and the Whitbread production budget was split between Laphroaig and Tormore to make them more viable. Warehousing was done at…Ben Nevis.

On 12 June 1986 Laphroaig narrowly escaped a real disaster when a Twin Otter airplane crashed nearby the distillery, killing the pilot and seriously injuring 11 more people aboard. An Aviation Safety report states 'However, the aircraft was not, at that time, over Port Ellen, but was in fact turning inland at very low level over Laphroaig. From overhead Laphroaig the aircraft settled on to a north westerly heading and very shortly afterwards crashed into rising ground that was obscured in hill fog, approximately 1 nm from the coast at a height of 360 feet amsl'. It must have made a deep impression on the people at Laphroaig and in Port Ellen.

When Colin Ross got back to Laphroaig, he thought the brand was lifting, but actually it was losing its status. The management asked him to increase production without actually knowing what that would do to the spirit. The recent improvements had cost so much money, that Ross only got in an extra spirit receiver, which allowed a production increase in that more spirit could be stored before being casked.

He then requested that spirit be put into tankers – which the warehouse man did. Colin recalled in an interview: 'They just ran a hose out to the tanker. Betty Campbell, the assistant excise officer was miffed – that was against all regulations because they didn't have proper permission'. This was the first time new make spirit from Laphroaig was tankered away. Before it had only been mature whisky tankered away for bottling. At the time the Customs & Excise Officers no longer lived at the premises but would come over regularly to do checks. The last C&E Officer to live at Laphroaig was Brice Whiteford. Both former Excise residences, Laphroaig House and Tigh-an-arbhair, were sold in the 1980s.

During his two-year-stint at Laphroaig, Ross entertained many foreign trade visitors, some coming from Cyprus, Japan and Australia. The Japanese Nikka Company was looking around at the

*1990s*

time to buy a Scottish distillery. They had visited Laphroaig several times to buy new make for their blends (another reason tankering started at the distillery). Laphroaig sold malt whisky to Yoichi during Colin's time.

Ross recalled: 'Sometimes I was as much a tour guide as a distillery manager.' In November 1988 a couple of Nikka's sales reps told Ross he would be working for them by Christmas. At the end of January 1989, Whitbread informed him that Nikka had asked for him to return to Ben Nevis distillery, which they acquired that same year. The Japanese must have been impressed with the 'tour guide', since they offered him a job as managing director, which he took in the second half of 1989.

## Iain Henderson

Whitbread sold all of its distilleries that year, but Laphroaig would not end up in Japanese hands this time. Allied Lyons now became the proud owner and rapidly appointed a man who is considered a legend in the whisky industry: Iain Henderson.

The new owner considered the sales of Laphroaig's single malt far too low. The newly appointed Iain Henderson was bluntly told to turn around the brand in no more than 12 months. Henderson could already look back upon an impressive career in the whisky industry, although he didn't start his working life at a distillery. Born in Edinburgh, having enjoyed a technical education, he moved to Fife after World War II and found employment in the Merchant Navy as a locomotive fitter on a steamboat. However, his wife preferred to have him on land and she persuaded him to apply for an engineering job at Bunnahabhain Distillery on Islay. It was the start of a long journey in the whisky world that took Henderson from the Speyside to the Lowlands and eventually brought him back to the island where it all started, but now at Laphroaig, whose whisky he had learned to enjoy in the late 1950s, when still with the merchant Navy.

In the second half of the 1950s Iain Henderson sailed on-board a ship heading from Glasgow to Australia. At the time single malts weren't as widespread as they are today. When the crew finally arrived in Port Pirie, a small Australian harbour town, the local bar surprisingly stocked two bottles of Laphroaig, albeit covered in cobwebs. According to the bartender the Australians didn't want to drink 'That TCP/Listerine stuff'. Iain and his fellow-sailors thought differently and emptied the bottles on the spot. So, in a way, Iain Henderson got reacquainted with Laphroaig, this time at its source.

The annual sales of Laphroaig Single Malt in 1989 were around 20,000 nine litre cases (one case being the equivalent of 12 bottles of 0.75 litre, totalling 180,000 litres). Although possessing a technical background, the concept of marketing was not alien to Henderson. He immediately sat down with then brand ambassador Jeremy Wetherhead and together with their advertising agency, they developed the basic idea of a brand loyalty program that would culminate in the inception of the Friends of Laphroaig five years later.

Thanks to the preliminary work of United Distillers (currently Diageo) in launching the Classic Six Malts in 1988, the worldwide interest in single malts gradually grew. Laphroaig always had been a strong brand and when Allied decided in 1991 to have an equivalent to the Classic Six, Laphroaig became part of the Caledonian Malts, further comprised of Miltonduff, Glendronach and Tormore (the latter eventually to be replaced by Scapa).

Henderson realised that customers became more and more interested in the people who made the product. He began traveling all over Europe, increasing brand awareness for Laphroaig. Being an eloquent speaker he was recognized and remembered wherever he went. Many distillery managers would follow in his footsteps to promote their own brand on a global stage.

In 1994 the name 'LAPHROAIG' appeared in big, bold letters on warehouse No 1. The painting was executed by Sam Graham and Donnie 'The Gunner' Stevenson who has been working as an operator at Laphroaig for more than two decades. Being a skilled carpenter, he made large wooden stencils for the curved letters.

To raise cash the blend Islay Mist was sold to MacDuff International in 1993. That year the distillery suffered a temporary setback when the pagoda roofs were destroyed by a fierce gale. Luckily they were restored in time for what might be called the ultimate highlight in Laphroaig's lifetime as well as Iain Henderson's career.

94

On 29 June 1994 HRH Prince Charles, who considers Laphroaig his favourite single malt, visited the distillery. Originally it would have been a flash visit, but HRH accidentally overshot the small airstrip on Islay and landed the plane slightly off the runway. The jet was damaged and could not return to Highgrove that day. Much to the delight of Henderson and his crew, HRH spent more than two hours at the distillery before a new plane arrived to bring him home.

HRH thoroughly enjoyed his visit to Laphroaig. He wanted to know everything about the process. In an interview with Jane Slade, for *Whisky Magazine*, Issue 12, Henderson recalled the visit as follows: 'He arrived with his private secretary Richard Ayling and detective Colin Tinning. They were a bit late because of the accident. I took His Royal Highness on a tour of the distillery and he was very impressive with his knowledge. He asked all the right questions and seemed to be enjoying himself. My wife Caroline prepared lunch. He had asked for poached salmon, salad and rice dishes. He wanted a buffet because there wasn't going to be time for a proper sit down. So he walked around with a dram in one hand and a plate in the other. He had asked to meet all the workers and their wives. He seemed genuinely interested in everyone and everything, and then said to me: 'I think this is a great place. I like the fact that you follow the traditional methods. Do not let anyone change it.'

The remarkable Royal Visit wasn't the only honour HRH bestowed upon Laphroaig. The distillery was given a Royal Warrant and Prince Charles signed two casks (1978 and 1983) from which the contents would later be sold and auctioned for charity. The proceeds from the 1978 cask went to the Cancer Relief Macmillan Fund and those of the 1983 cask to Erskine Hospital. Prince Charles chose both recipients. The head of the 1983 cask can be seen on a wall at Erskine Hospital in Glasgow. This institution cares for the ex-Service men and women of Scotland. The 1978 cask can be seen as part of a historical display inside the entrance of Warehouse 1.

The year 1994 witnessed another important event. Allied Lyons became Allied-Domecq, through which merger a British-Spanish company now owned Laphroaig.

In 1991 Iain Henderson and Jeremy Weatherhead developed a unique brand loyalty program in close cooperation with International Marketing Promotions (IMP), their PR Agency at the time. It would culminate in the launch of The Friends of Laphroaig club in 1994, sustained by a monthly newsletter and – in later years – a website inviting lovers of Laphroaig to become a member. In 1999 VPH Digital took over IMP's role and has been developing new functionalities for the Friends ever since.

*1990s*

Standing (left to right): William Campbell, Ruaraidh MacIntyre, Allan Hyslop, John Logan, Hamish Gillespie, Billy Johnston, Donnie Stevenson, Harry Paterson, Nigel MacTaggart, Michael Heads, David Adams, Iain Henderson, Ian Hallam

Kneeling/seated (left to right): John Campbell, Andrew Hamilton, Neil McDougal, Dan Heads, Donald Campbell, Alex Gunn, Alex Livingstone, Philip Ayres, Ted Burkenshaw, Alex Woodrow, Eddie Morris, Jack Dunford, James McGregor, Gordon McKechnie

Friends have certain privileges and are given lifetime lease on a piece of land on the grounds of Laphroaig. When visiting the distillery Friends can collect their rent in the form of a miniature of 10-year-old Laphroaig. This loyalty program became an instant success and has been running for 21 consecutive years in 2015. Chapter 5 is specially dedicated to the Friends of Laphroaig, all 700,000 of them and still counting!

In 1995 the product line was expanded with a cask strength version of 10-year-old Laphroaig. A 30-year-old followed as well as two vintages (1976 and 1977). A 40-year-old was launched in 2001, the oldest single malt Laphroaig expression ever. For this purpose the distillery had to buy back casks that had been previously sold to independent bottler Duncan Taylor in 1961 by Bessie. At the time both Duncan Taylor and Laphroaig were in American hands. The total output of the 40-year-old in 2001 was 4,000 bottles. This whisky rapidly became a collector's item.

During Henderson's management the malting floors and the kiln furnaces underwent modifications. This was necessary to implement a heat-reclamation system. The draff dryer chimney had been demolished in 1994 and henceforth the draff would be sold wet. The turning of the malt with shovels, taking several hands at the same time, was replaced by an electrical turner that could be operated by one man. 'The justification for using 200-year-old technology is part heritage, part PR and part common sense. It helps us keep that edge', commented Henderson about those changes.

In 2002 Iain Henderson retired at the age of 65, following Allied's company policy not to retain employees above that age. With much regret Mr Laphroaig changed Islay for his home grounds in Fife. In the same year 130,000 cases of Laphroaig were sold (1,170,000 litres).

## Robin Shields

Allied did ask Henderson however to help finding a suitable successor. For a short time John Campbell, a born and bread Ileach, recruited by Iain in 1994, acted as manager, until Robin Shields was appointed at the end of 2002. Shields, an Englishman from Yorkshire with 25 years in the brewing industry under his belt, modestly took over the position of Iain Henderson, after having completed a six-week in-company training course in Speyside. When he was asked by Martine Nouet, writing for *Whisky Magazine* at the time, about his plans for the future of Laphroaig he replied: 'I was brought here as a guardian of the past to preserve the heritage. At the same time, I must be mindful of the present.' When approached by us in 2014 Robin Shields reflected upon his short stay with the following email:

*I was only at Laphroaig for just over two years, and it was my only experience of the whisky industry. At the interview I was advised that people take the job for a lifetime or they only last 18 months. I am obviously one of the latter. I had always had a bit of a dream about running a distillery on an island, so I am very pleased to have achieved the ambition. However for me the reality was not the same as the dream. The people at the distillery and on the island were very welcoming, but being part of big corporate life with Allied Domecq, and yet being based on a remote site did not work well for me. Allied to the other facts that I developed a passionate distaste for midges, and also my father in law was terminally ill which necessitated frequent laborious trips away from the island for my wife, the decision to resign was taken, before our house on the mainland was sold.*

It was nice to have been involved in the first special single cask bottling (a 17-year-old) for the Feis Ile 2004. I learned a lot about applying labels by hand and hand filling of 250 bottles. I am glad to see that in John Campbell's capable hands that such marketing and brand extensions have gone from strength to strength.'

A fact that Shields did not mention, and witness to his modesty, is the launch of Laphroaig Quarter Cask during his short time. This whisky, matured for a series of years in ex-bourbon barrels, was poured into 125 litre so-called quarter casks to mature for another seven months. Because of the smaller size of this type of cask, the whisky matures at a more rapid pace, since the amount of wood surface to which the whisky is exposed is larger than that of an ex-bourbon barrel (holding approximately 250 litres when modified). Given the age of the bottled whisky, distilling must have taken place when Iain Henderson managed the distillery, so inevitably his spirit echoes in the taste of this dram.

## John Campbell

In 2005 Allied Domecq decided to sell out and the giants in the whisky industry sharpened their knives for a battle of bidding. Fortune Brands, with its subsidiary Beam Global Spirits & Wine, was the lucky winner. After 30 years Laphroaig returned into American hands, this time to be flanked by two legendary bourbons: Jim Beam and Maker's Mark. Robin Shields, eventually more a brewer than a distiller, listened to the tolling of the brewing bells and returned to his first love, to be succeeded by a man whose clan has been connected to Islay since 1615 and to Laphroaig from the very start. On 19 January 2006 at 2:35 pm, John Campbell was appointed and thus became the youngest distillery manager on Islay at the time.

*2000s*

John set himself a personal goal when he took up the job as distillery manager in 2006. He wanted to turn the distillery into a better place for sustainable success. It should be a team effort where people could exchange jobs and the running of the operation would not depend on an individual person. To reach this goal John created a solid management team that currently consists of four people. Besides himself they are Vicky Stevens, David Livingstone and Caroline Morris. The following plan was executed over the years. Each department would be looked at and its employees were taken on a journey with a member of the management team. The work was broken down into steps and each different area was examined to see what could be improved. This is an on-going process. Between 2006 and 2015 the following changes have taken place.

## Equipment and Procedures

As of 2006 the phenol content of the malted barley has been increased. This is enhanced by spraying the peat in the shed, so that its moisture content stays up and the peat is usable longer. From March 2006 on Laphroaig was running as a 24/7 operation plant with only a few weeks per year shut down for maintenance, usually in the summer and over Christmas. Today they are running 24/7 for 33 weeks per year. The kiln floors were replaced in 2007. In 2008 a new boiler was installed which made a huge difference in efficiency and was a kick-start to a whole series of improvements. The old one was 30 years old, had only 100 psi, 'a nightmare, at the end of its days', according to engineer Nigel MacTaggart.

In 2009 three fans per floor were installed in the bayside maltings windows. Before that modification took place, ventilation could only be controlled by adjusting the windows manually. The malt chariot capacity was increased to make laying the floor more efficient, resulting in fewer trips up & down. A funnel was made to keep the malt going straight down to the lower floor from the steeps, removing the need for the maltsters to shovel the malt into the opening.

'The 'smallest railroad in Scotland' also called 'the peat bogie' was decommissioned in 2012. The little train broke down frequently and became inefficient, despite its nostalgic value. Now the peat enters the kilns via a big hopper and a conveyor belt transports it to the fires, which saves a lot of time. The entrance road that leads from the main road to the distillery was retarred in 2009. In 2010 a brand new lift was built outside between warehouse 1 and 7.

The condemned lift in warehouse 1 was removed; the upper two floors of warehouse 1 have been restored and are now back in use after many years of lying idle. It illustrates the huge production growth and the need for extra storage space. Furthermore the #1 spirit still's base was renewed. In 2011 a new ventilation system was installed in the still house, with pipes blowing cold air on the operators' station. A simple but ingenious form of air conditioning.

In order to warm up the malt barns, in 2012 an air pipe from the kiln was installed. A couple of valves from the radiator can be operated, pinching a bit of the (unpeated) hot air that goes through the kiln. This is done especially in winter, when temperatures drop too much for germination to start properly. That same year the cladding roofs on warehouses 10A and 10B were replaced, as well as the roof on the mill area. The latter was done mainly for health and safety reasons, since the old roof still contained asbestos. Also in 2012 Laphroaig changed from dried yeast to liquid yeast. Mauri is still the supplier and was willing to invest in necessary equipment such as a liquid yeast tank and pump. It was a win-win situation. Mauri found it easier to ship it in and at Laphroaig the guys were happy that they need not lift the heavy 25 kg bags anymore. Touch screens were installed for charging and discharging the stills, which increased the level of automation.

In 2013 a new spirit safe was installed, while in 2014 the windows in the malt barns were changed again. The old windows were a swivel type; the new ones have two doors. According to malt-man Barry MacAffer 'it is a massive improvement, allows a lot more air through the malt barns and it is easier to control the floors in combination with the fans. The three fans per floor can all operate individually if needed. A nice breeze is even better, with the sea air. I love that distinct smell of the barley.'

2014 also witnessed a new roof on the still house, which improved ventilation. All still man-hole doors were renewed, now carrying the name 'Laphroaig' instead of 'Arch. Macmillan - Edinburgh'. Bigger pumps are in place to fill the stills faster. They are running the same as before, but the run is five hours and twenty five minutes instead of six and a half hours. The cut is still done manually.

Assistant Manager David Livingstone explained as follows: 'We did not change anything in the way it is processed, but filling times, heating and pre-heating are done more efficiently. When you remove waste time that has a big impact. We came from 2.2 million litres in 2006 and managed to produce 3.1 million litres in 2013. The estimate for 2014 is 3.4 million. We managed to do that without increasing the existing capacity. To give you an example, if you save only five minutes per day by streamlining operations, you might be talking about 20,000 extra litres of Laphroaig annually.'

Two more examples were given by John Campbell: 'After the wash distillation, it took over an hour to empty the still, refill it, then an hour to get it boiling. By making that process more efficient, we were able to make 500,000-600,000 litres more per year.'

*Gordon MacLennan making the cut.*

There was more capacity in the fermenters, so now that is being used by changing the mash cycles. It was one 8.5 tonne mash producing wort for one washback (and then about four wash charges). Now two 5.5 tonne mashes produce enough for one washback and then about five wash charges result.

The pipeline for the effluent plant was improved by placing a ducktail on the end, which helps with the dispersion into Laphroaig Bay. It is twice as efficient and has a lower environmental impact. The water supply is still the same but due to some damming work the capacity is increased.

Laphroaig changes barley varieties as needed, mainly because the farmers have made the shift. Most draff is returned to the mainland. All Islay distilleries have increased their output 'and there are only so many cows on the island to eat the draff', according to John.

With his team he is also looking at sustainable energy sources: waves, wind and solar energy. 'Nothing is reliable enough right now to implement and we cannot afford to drop production'.

## Personnel and Visitors

Today there are 33 employees. The visitor centre has seen the largest growth of personnel between 2006 and 2015. One of the causes might well be the new ferry infrastructure, which helped increase the number of visitors to the island.

When Vicky Stevens became responsible for the visitor centre, one of her first moves was to open the doors for seven days a week between March and December. In January and February visitors are welcome from Monday to Friday. The following numbers illustrate the impact on this part of the work force. In 2008 Vicky had 1.5 staff members; in 2015, five full time and four part time. Over the same period the amount of annual visitors grew from 7,000 to 23,000. The visitors program is largely extended and currently five standard tours a day are on offer, as well as four premium visits, among which the Distillers Warehouse Experience and the Water to Whisky Tour.

The entire visitor centre was redone and now has a small museum attached to the shop as well as a special tasting room. Laphroaig was awarded Best Whisky Distillery Tour three times at the Drammies. The distillery received the Icons of Whisky award for Whisky Visitor Attraction of the Year in 2014 and Best Visitor Attraction Award in Scotland in 2015.

The Friends of Laphroaig has grown to a staggering group of more than 700,000 members from 190 different nationalities and still counting. A visiting Friend can borrow a GPS tracker and a pair of green Wellies to go off to the moors across from the distillery and find the exact spot of his or her plot. Free flags are available for those who want to nationalise their square foot. The website has been updated and Facebook and Twitter usage has increased tremendously over the past eight years.

*The team at Laphroaig (joining date in parentheses) from left to right, standing: Vicky Stevens (07-06-2008), Barry MacAffer (15-09-2011), Graham Holyoake (25-08-2008), Sam Johnston (01-03-2012), William Campbell (16-04-1979), Gregor McTavish (28-01-2007), Michael Bonar (04-06-2010), David McLean (12-06-2006), Gordon MacLennan (22-09-2010), James McGregor (20-10-1975), David Adams (08-04-1975), Peter MacTaggart (08-05-2006), Billy Johnston (01-06-1989), Arthur Holyoake (12-08-2002), David Livingstone (02-10-2002), Nigel MacTaggart (06-02-1989), Stevie Ewing (13-05-2014), James Deane (25-04-2012), John Campbell (14-11-1994), Danielle McKerrell (11-03-2010), Bryony Boyd (04-01-2011), Debbie Cameron (06-12-2010).*
*Seated: Andrew Hamilton (06-02-1984), Emma Boyle (09-05-2005), Caroline Morris (19-03-1990), Jenny Husthwaite (27-02-2012), Christianne MacGregor (01-09-2014).*
*Not pictured: Jennifer Gillies (27-02-2012), Alan Hyslop (12-05-1980), Sean McFarlane (04-01-2010), John Mcniven (29-10-1984), Donnie Stevenson (05-01-1994).*

All in all, it is busier and busier on the site. The employees have been asked to do more different things, have a broader scope and job, which has affected everyone working at the distillery. 2014 had record production levels and 2015 expects to do the same. John Campbell has achieved the goal he set in 2006 and credited the entire team with it. However, it will be an on-going process for years to come.

## Japanese ownership

In 2014 the takeover of Laphroaig's parent company Beam Global by the Japanese drinks giant Suntory was ratified. Now a new period under new ownership is dawning. Laphroaig's long-standing track record in the USA, with sales even during Prohibition, is one of the unique assets Suntory inherits from a company founded 200 years ago by two brothers, whose surname still is shown on the bottle: Johnston.

The most important asset however, may be that remarkable group of dedicated people that combines 480 years of working experience in 2015, whilst creating one of the most distinctive drinks in the world: Laphroaig Scotch single malt whisky.

Let's have a look at how Laphroaig is made today and meet some of these great people.

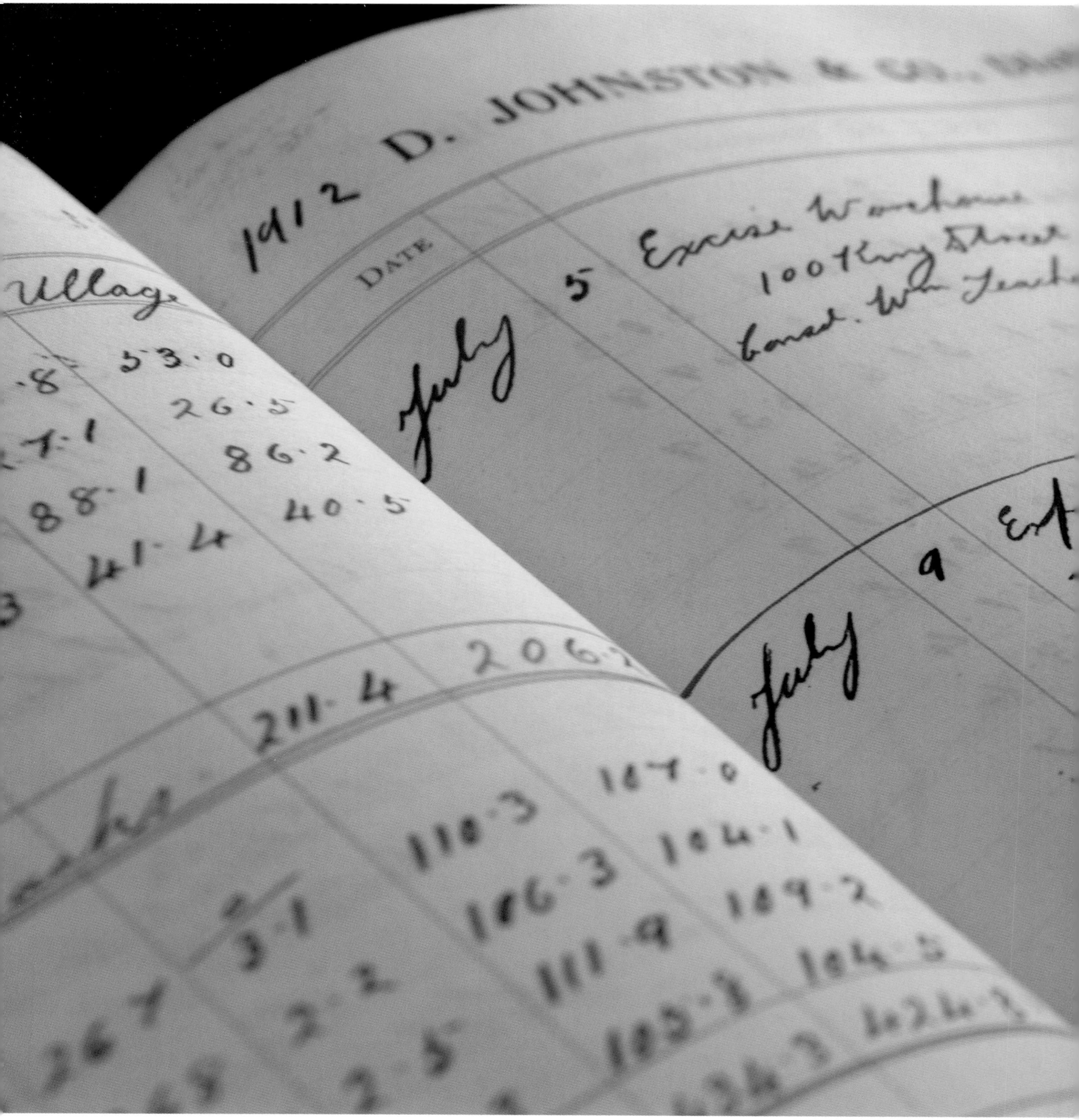

1912 D. JOHNSTON & Co., Distillers

Ullage

.8     53·0
.7·1     26·5
88·1     86·2
41·4     40·5
3

211·4     206·2

July     5   Excise Warehouse
                100 King Street
                Const. Wm Jenkins

July     9   Ext

3·1     110·3     107·0
2·2     106·3     104·1
2·5     111·9     109·2
          105·3     104·5
26·7
59         434·3     104·8

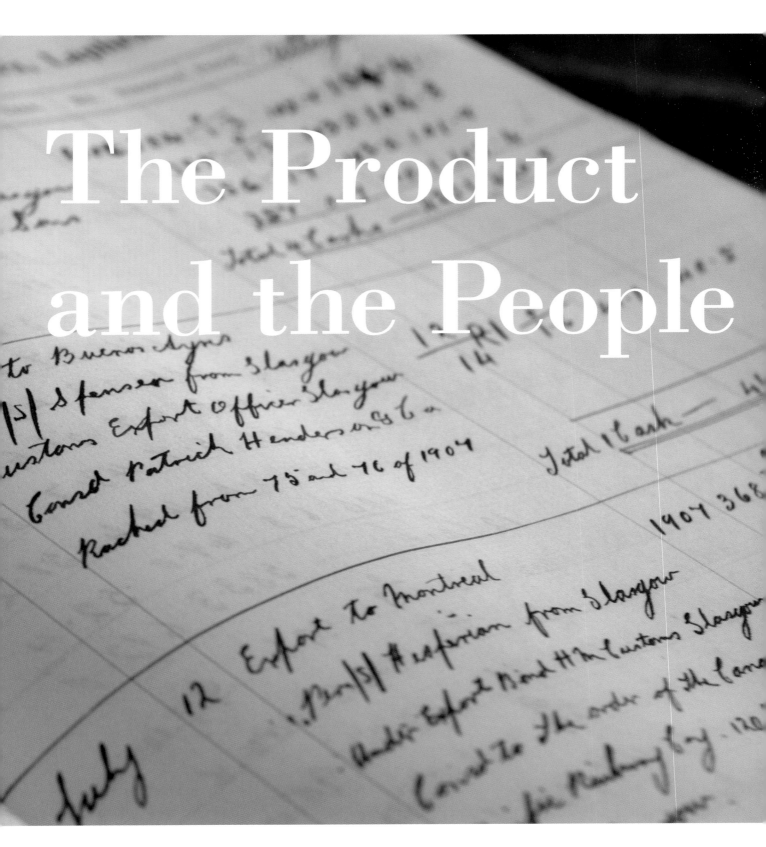

# The Product
# and the People

# The Product
# and the People

The production process of single malt whisky can be divided into the following seven steps: Malting & Milling, Mashing, Fermentation, Distillation, Filling, Maturation and Bottling. Only three ingredients are used: water, barley and yeast.

Laphroaig currently employs 33 people to get the job done, 24/7. The distillery closes for a few weeks in the summer and over the Christmas holidays. Before we get acquainted with some of these fine craftsmen and women, let's have a look at the raw materials of which Laphroaig is made and what other materials are essential in the process.

## Water

Water that streams through relatively light soil takes on many more minerals than water that makes its way over a rocky terrain. Each *terroir* contains different minerals. Some examples illustrate that nicely: the granite in part of the Speyside is very hard and contains hardly any minerals, resulting in very pure water. In the Northern Highlands, for instance around the village of Tain, the water is rich in minerals since it ascends through layers of limestone. On the Isle of Islay the water runs its course to the distillery over peat bogs that mainly consist of decayed seaweed and heather.

The source that feeds Laphroaig is the Kilbride Reservoir, securely closed off by the Kilbride Dam. In its turn this reservoir is fed by Steins Dam, a huge catchment area covering 800 hectares. Loch na Beinne Brice can also be used to supply the Kilbride Reservoir.

The contents of the reservoir are primarily used as process water. Cooling water comes from the overflow of the dam and finds its way to the distillery via a stream (opposite page). The colour is brown, coming from the peat through which the water has percolated before reaching the distillery. The peat overlays quartzite rocks. The water is highly acidic, but there is little reaction with the underlying stone, so the mineral content of the water is low. There are no phenols in Laphroaig's water, as was confirmed in a report from Munton & Fison Ltd, dated 7 February 1967 to Bessie Williamson Campbell.

## Barley

Of all the grains, malted barley renders the most flavours to the eventual whisky. Barley also contains a high level of starch. When the barley is malted, natural enzymes are formed, which help to convert the starch into fermentable sugars. Generally speaking we distinguish two types of barley: two-row, with one row of seeds on each side of the halm; and six-row, with three rows of seeds on each side. The variety of barley used at Laphroaig changes as needed.

Cultivating new barley varieties is a continuous process. Barley is prone to picking up fungi, even barley that was originally resistant. New forms are tested in the laboratory of the National Institute of Agricultural Botany (NIAB), whose headquarters is located in Cambridge, England. Testing takes at least two years before the new variety can be placed on the UK National List. It is also possible to have a new type of barley added to the EU Common Catalogue of Varieties. Therefore official tests are required in all EU Member States. If a new variety performs well, the whisky industry might exchange it for its previous barley.

Currently 20% is malted on-site. The remaining 80% is malted conforming to exact specifications at Port Ellen Maltings, a couple of miles to the west. The malt storage facility at the distillery can hold 284 tonnes.

As early as Ian Hunter's reign, Laphroaig did not produce enough malted barley for its entire production. Old purchase ledgers show figures relating to the purchase of malted barley elsewhere. Bessie Williamson continued purchasing from third parties, as proven by correspondence between her and James Buchanan & Co., in a letter from 1966.

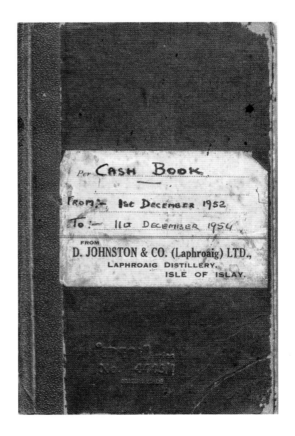

## Peat

Although peat itself is not an actual ingredient as such to make whisky, its smoke during the drying of the barley heavily influences the taste. Peat smoke contains little particles called phenols. Their level is measured in parts per million (ppm).

Laphroaig owns peat fields that stretch over Machrie Moor, close to the tiny airport of Islay. All peat is hand cut, usually in April and May.

First the top grass is cut about six to eight inches and laid over the fields where peat was cut the previous year. The first actual peat cut, about 3/4 metre of land, is not as decayed as the deeper layer and produces more smoke than heat. The second peat cut, also 3/4 metre, is more compact and decayed, resulting in more heat and less smoke when burned. The cut peat is left to dry on the lands and transported to the peat shed on the distillery grounds in August. Laphroaig needs approximately 200 tonnes each year.

The ppm level of phenols is a deciding factor in the character of the eventual whisky. In 1967 Bessie Williamson requested Munton & Fison to test Laphroaig's malt. Their report mentioned that the difference in the moisture level between different layers might play a part in the actual peatiness of whisky. Smoke is more important than heat when kilning the malt. At Laphroaig the peat fires are sprayed with water, to increase and gently cool off the smoke, which leads to the intense peaty character of its single malt.

After the distillery expansion of 1972, more additional malt came from central malting companies. Before 1972, ppm could have been around 40 to 45. Originally the malt that Moray Firth Maltsters delivered was nearly non-peated (4 ppm) until Irish Maltsters developed a new technique for malting highly peated barley (about 30 ppm) on a large scale. The phenolic content increased but not to the level of Laphroaig's own maltings from the

*Sam Johnston adding peat to the kiln fire.*

years before 1972. Irish Maltsters continued to supply malted barley well into the 1980s, though Laphroaig still did not have a phenol level of 45 to 50ppm. According to the records the level had dropped to 25 ppm in 1982.

When Allied bought Laphroaig, the level was supposed to be at 25 ppm but rarely reached that height, even with in-house peating. Irish Maltsters couldn't even reach higher than 10 to 12 ppm over all their shipments in 1991, so they lost the contract that year due to the low ppm levels. The Concordat of Islay Distillers was drawn up and signed in 1987. It was an agreement between Port Ellen Maltings and the distillers of Islay and Jura that they would take at least a portion of their malt from Port Ellen Maltings. In essence it saved the maltings from closure and assured the local distilleries a source of customer-specific malt. Laphroaig participated in the Concordat when it was started and Port Ellen Maltings have been supplying Laphroaig since.

When Laphroaig arranged for the first shipments under the Concordat, the maltings could only reach around 25 ppm and had great difficulty creating a heavier peat flavour. In 1997 Port Ellen Maltings perfected their method and could deliver malted barley with a level of 45-50 ppm, as requested by then master blender Robert Hicks.

The current ppm level of Laphroaig's malted barley is higher than that coming in from Port Ellen, and has even increased since 2006. One has to bear in mind however that when distilled, the phenol levels drop dramatically. During maturation they drop even further.

## Yeast

Yeast is a single-celled fungus that can rapidly mulitply under the influence of oxygen. This is called aerobic fermentation. In addition, yeast can convert sugar into alcohol and carbon dioxide, which is referred to as anaerobic fermentation. The chemical equation for the anaerobic fermentation of glucose is $C_6H_{12}O_6$ (glucose) $\longrightarrow$ $2C_2H_5OH$ (ethanol) + $2CO_2$. The Latin name for yeast is *Saccharomyces cerevisiae* (saccharo = sweet; myces = mold). There are at present between 700 and 1000 different known species. However, they do not all have the same ability to convert sugar into alcohol.

Yeast is found on plants, in the air, in the ground, in and on humans and animals. Wild yeasts in nature proliferate spontaneously but are preferably not used in the production of whisky. Most Scottish distillers use a cultured yeast that is supplied in lyophilized form by commercial yeast producers. There are three types: distiller's yeast, baker's yeast and brewer's yeast. One type provides more flavours, and the other more alcohol. Initially the Scottish distillers used a mix of the three. Creating a balance was therefore important. In the past Laphroaig also used brewer's yeast, from Burton-on-Trent. It was solid, difficult to work with, it had a disagreeable smell and a tendency to break in pieces. Nowadays most distilleries in the industry purchase only distiller's yeast, especially the variants Mauri and Quest.

Since yeast contributes significantly to the flavours of whisky, the interchangeability of yeast cultures is very limited. Use of different yeast strains can change the taste of the end product. Laphroaig therefore sticks exclusively to Mauri yeast cultures, ordered from a commercial production plant in Hull, England.

## Copper

The material from which Laphroaig's distinctive stills are built has a long pedigree. Copper is the first metal with which mankind got acquainted. In the beginning it was used in its pure form but later it was mixed with pewter, resulting in the alloy bronze. Its name is derived from the Latin *aes cyprium*, meaning 'ore from Cyprus'. This Greek/Turkish island used to be a famous place to dig for copper in ancient times. Copper is known as a transitional metal. In its pure form it is not overabundant in nature, but is found more often as a copper-containing mineral. Examples are covelite, malachite, bornite and chalcopyrite. Copper ore is currently won mainly in parts of South America and the USA.

The first use of copper goes back more than 10,000 years, which was proven by excavations in current Iraq and South-Jordan, where archaeologists stumbled upon King Solomon's copper mines. That discovery was made in Kirbat-en-Nahas – Arabic for 'ruins of copper'. In ancient times copper was primarily used for tools, weapons, jewellery and mirrors.

The whisky industry wouldn't exist without copper. Various tools of the trade are made of it. The spirit safe, parts of the pipes and valves needed for transporting the liquid from and to the wash and spirit still are made of copper. The basic design is in use in modern day distilleries and has hardly been modified in 400 years. Copper is ideal for distilling since it is an excellent conductor and easy to work with for a smith. It is also a very good catalyst, interacting easily with the spirit, resulting in various chemical reactions, by which unwanted sulphuric components will disappear.

A pot still basically consists of four copper parts:

1. the pot, in which fermented wash or low wines are heated;
2. the swan neck, through which the alcohol fumes ascend;
3. the lyne arm or lye pipe, guiding the alcohol fumes to the condenser;
4. the condenser – a tube-and-shell or an old-fashioned worm tub, in which the fumes cool down and become an oily liquid.

The various sizes of all those parts of the distilling equipment all influence the eventual taste of the whisky in different manners. For instance the angle of the lyne arm plays its part. Small copper kettles with short necks interact more intensely with the spirit than larger ones with long necks. A small pot still usually produces a heavier spirit, whereas from a large pot still a lighter variety emerges. This has nothing to do with the quality of the eventual whisky but with the body.

Pot stills are heated in different manners: indirectly from coils with steam heating or directly fired under the still. The latter method can cause caramelisation on the bottom of the still. That also influences the taste and aroma. With the help of so-called rummagers – a kind of chain that is dragged over the bottom – the burnt residue is scraped off, including miniscule amounts of copper. In earlier days direct firing was the only method but indirect heating increased in popularity after its introduction around 1960.

Due to the endless stop-start cycle of heating-cooling-cleaning-heating and so forth the copper wears out. That doesn't happen evenly and that is why a pot still is seldom replaced in its entirety. It is more customary to change parts that are in need of replacement. The lifespan of a pot still is approximately 40 years.

The still comes in three basic forms: lantern, pear and onion. All forms are used throughout the industry and usually the spirit still differs from the wash still in a distillery. Pairs of the same stills are nearly always similar in shape, with exceptions such as Laphroaig, with one spirit still that is significantly larger than the other three. Laphroaig's wash stills are onion-shaped, the spirit stills more lantern-shaped. They used to be made at Abercrombie in Alloa. Currently the stills, and parts thereof are manufactured at Forsyth's of Rothes, Speyside.

LAPHROIG
STILL

## Wood

The cask heavily influences the flavour of the eventual whisky. It is made of either American or European oak, since this type of wood has a few important characteristics. It does not break when heated; hence it can be bent into shape more easily. Furthermore it is porous and allows the liquid inside to seep into the wood.

The cask breathes, oxidising the contents, also forming part of its character. About 2% evaporates each year and is called The Angels' Share. The ideal age for an oak tree to be transformed into a cask is between 80 and 90 years.

Temperature changes throughout the year will cause the maturing fluid to expand in summer and contract in winter. During this process the liquid gains colour, flavours and aromas. A limited maturation time will render a young, raw and rather fierce whisky; too long a stay in the cask may turn the contents into 'oak-juice'. The company decides when casks are ready for bottling, keeping in mind that by law spirit must mature a minimum of three years in oak casks before it can be called whisky.

Through the ages different types of oak casks were used, for instance rum casks, bourbon barrels, sherry butts, port pipes and wine casks, either made of the American white oak *(Quercus alba)* or the European red oak *(Quercus robur)*.

The Scottish whisky distillers have a preference for pre-used casks that impart the desired colour, flavour and aroma over a longer period of time than new wood. Laphroaig predominantly uses casks that formerly held bourbon.

After four to five years of service in the bourbon industry, the barrel (or cask if you prefer) will be used up to three more times in Scotland, typically for 10 to 12 year periods. After that it is exhausted and the remaining wood is put to use as barbecue fuel or garden furniture. From acorn to retired cask takes a life span of 120 years.

*Sean MacFarlane sampling the grist.*

*Alan Hyslop at the mash tun.*

## How Laphroaig Is Made Today

The majority of distilleries in Scotland buy their barley malted on spec from one of the large commercial maltsters. Hence this early stage in the making of whisky usually escapes the eye of the distillery visitor. Laphroaig is one of the very few distilleries that maintains an old-fashioned malting floor, albeit that only a small percentage is malted on-site - the amount of malted barley needed, exceeds the capacity of the malting floors. It is a truly unique feature and the perfect place to start a tour. The maltings are one of the oldest buildings of the distillery. When the malting floors and kilns were modified in the mid 1990s, the workmen found a brick dated 1840!

## Malting & Milling

Barley has to be malted to convert its starch into soluble sugars, from which alcohol can be gained later in the process, during fermentation. First the barley is soaked in water in the three steeping tanks, for a duration of 51 hours with air rests between each of three soakings. Ideally the moisture content will be around 45% at the end of steeping. The grains are subsequently spread out on the malting floor to germinate. During the winter germination takes up to seven days and in summer four to six days, depending on the ambient temperature. The malt has to be turned manually to aerate the slightly sticky mass that would otherwise become overheated and scorched.

peat. Kilning takes around 17 hours using peat smoke, followed by 17-20 hours drying with hot air.

As soon as the malt is dried, it is transported to one of the eight malt bins to rest. One week's worth of malting will fill one malt bin. Malt from Port Ellen Maltings is brought in each day. After the rest period, a combination of the malt from Laphroaig and malt from Port Ellen will be transported to the mill via a conveyor-belt. Laphroaig uses a Porteus mill. When milled the malted barley consists of three parts, from coarse to fine: husk (25%), grits (60%) and flour (15%). This ratio is important for the next stage. Too much husk will mean a lower percentage of soluble sugars; too much flour will cause cloying of the substance in the mash tun.

## Mashing

The mixture of milled components is called grist. At most, 16.5 tonnes can be stored before use. Laphroaig's heating tanks  feed the mash tun and can hold a maximum of 42,000 litres of water. The 5.5 tonnes of grist in the mash tun will be charged with hot water three times. The first charge consists of 24,500 litres at 64.5°C (148.1°F), the second one of 14,800 litres and the third of 16,000 litres both at 85°C (185°F). A full mash cycle takes about four hours.

Furthermore it prevents the sprouts getting entangled.

When germination continues for too long, the sprouted grains start eating the sugars, which will result in a lower yield of alcohol than desired. The maltman's skills prevent that. He knows exactly when the green malt is ready for drying. To stop germination the 'green malt', as it is called in this stage, has to be dried in a kiln, a kind of oven whose chimney is crowned with a pagoda. Kilns can be fuelled by coal, oil or peat. The latter fuel is imperative to Laphroaig and responsible for its pungent, smoky flavour, caused by the phenols in the

The sugars in the grist are dissolved in the water, which is drained off through a huge sieve in the bottom of the vessel via the underback to the fermenting vessel, or washback. The liquid is now called 'wort'. Two 5.5 tonne mashes produce enough wort to fill one washback. The residue in the mash tun is called draff. It is sold to a local contractor and used for cattle feed on Islay and the Kintyre peninsula.

## Fermentation

Whereas most distilleries have separate mash houses and tun rooms, at Laphroaig it is an open floor plan. Mashing and brewing (fermenting) equipment basically are in the same room and can relatively easily be operated by one person. Yeast is added to the washback, which is stored before use in a liquid yeast tank near the mash tun. Each of the six washbacks at Laphroaig has a capacity of 52,800 litres.

The initial fermentation temperature is 18-19° C (64.4-66.2° F), but during the process it will rise to 33° C (91.4° F). At that point the temperature is regulated to prevent over-heating. Fermenting takes 55 hours in total. It is a turbulent process, with heavy frothing and bubbling, kept under control by using rotating fans inside the top of the sealed washbacks. The remaining sweet liquid is called wash, contains approximately 8.5% alcohol by volume and can be compared with a strong kind of beer. Up to this stage the production resembles that of brewing beer, hence the term 'brewer' for the person who operates the tun room.

## Distillation

The wash is pumped to the still house to be distilled twice. The first round of distillation takes place in a wash still, of which Laphroaig has three of identical size. They can hold approximately 12,000 litres each, but are charged at 83.5% of their capacity (10,500 litres). Steam pans inside the still provide the heat. This method prevents burnt residue, so no rummagers are required. At Laphroaig the stills were direct-fired until 1967.

Since alcohol has a lower boiling point than water, it evaporates earlier. The alcohol fumes rise through the neck and the slightly ascending lyne arm of the still into a cooler, called a condenser. The result is a liquid containing approximately 22% alcohol, referred to as 'low wines' and is caught in a vessel called the low wines receiver. The leftovers in the wash still are called pot ale. They are pumped to the effluent plant next to the mash house to be treated before poured into Laphroaig Bay, following environmental regulations. A typical run of the wash stills takes five hours.

The low wines are transferred to the spirit still for a second distillation. The spirit stills are heated internally by steam coils. Laphroaig runs three of them with a capacity of 4,700 litres each and one with double capacity, spirit still No. 1 or the Big Still. The second round demands much more from the stillman's skills than the first one. The first part of the distillate is called 'foreshots' or heads. It mainly contains the poisonous methyl alcohol. For 45 minutes the stillman lets the foreshots run back into the low wines receiver, to be redistilled with the next batch. Then he switches the tap to the spirits receiver and catches the heart of the run (also called middle cut) for about two and

a half hours for the small stills and three and a half hours for the Big Still, after which respective periods he returns the tap to the low wines receiver. The third part called 'feints' or tails, is not wanted either, since it contains fusel oils and heavier alcohols that can influence the taste of the eventual whisky in a negative way. They run for about two hours and will be redistilled in the next batch.

A so-called spirit safe is used to separate foreshots and feints from the heart of the run. This is a device with which the stillman can measure the density of the alcohol by means of a hydrometer and a thermometer. Originally the spirit safes were installed by Excise men with the purpose of preventing the stillman from 'stealing' spirit. They became widely used starting in 1823, coinciding with new legislation on acquiring a license to distil. Several distilleries use an automated device to catch the heart of the run. At Laphroaig it has always been left to the stillman to decide when to switch the tap. The leftovers, called 'spent lees' are pumped to the effluent plant and will eventually end up in Laphroaig Bay as well.

The liquid collected from the heart of the run is now waiting in the spirit receiver, ready to be pumped to the filling room. Meanwhile the hot water from the condensers is fed into a heat-exchange system that produces hot air for drying the malted barley in the kilns. Nothing goes to waste.

## Maturation

The white spirit that cannot be named whisky yet comes off the stills at 68% ABV and is diluted in the filling store to 63.5% before being put into oak casks. It has to mature for at least three years before it can legally be called whisky.

Today Laphroaig uses primarily first fill ex-bourbon American oak barrels from Kentucky distillers Maker's Mark and Jim Beam, but does experiment with other types of casks. One famous experiment that turned into a readily available expression of Laphroaig is the Quarter Cask.

Since its inception Laphroaig's warehouses were increased in numbers from the original one to the current eight. Part of them are old-style dunnage warehouses with an earthen floor, part are modern racked ones with concrete floors. They are oddly numbered: 1, 7, 8, 9, 9a, 10a, 10b and 11. Together they can store approximately 55,000 casks.

About 66% of the annual output of 3.4 million litres is kept for maturing as a single malt, of which 70% matures on site and 30% is tankered away to the former Long John site in Glasgow where the spirit is filled into barrels. The remaining 33% of the yearly production is destined to go to the blenders, who favour Laphroaig as a strong backbone. Among them are famous well-established brands like Ballantine's, Chivas, J&B, Black Grouse and Islay Mist.

## Bottling

All mature whisky is shipped to the mainland where it is bottled in Glasgow, from where it is distributed worldwide.

## Craftsmanship

Each step in the process of making Laphroaig requires special craftsmanship. It is not uncommon in the whisky industry that newly employed people start at the beginning of the process and work their way up to the top. John Campbell, for example, started at Laphroaig as a warehouseman, having previously been a self-employed fisherman. Via the maltings he became assistant brewer, then brewer and eventually was appointed distillery manager.

At Laphroaig various people are trained to switch jobs, for instance between working in the mash house and in the stillhouse. This is a necessity, since production runs 24/7 and the men have to work in shifts.

Retired warehouseman Eddie Morris started 52 years ago as a 15-year-old farm hand for Bessie Williamson before treading in his father's footsteps, who worked for 30 years in Laphroaig's warehouses. James McGregor, employed by Laphroaig for 40 years, started as a painter in warehouse 1 and 2, went to the malt barns, the still house and the drying of draff before returning to the warehouse again.

The dedicated men and women who work together to create and present your dram of Laphroaig, are a worthy bunch altogether. Time to meet some interesting characters up close and personal.

*David McLean and James McGregor moving casks in the filling store.*

# John Campbell

Joined Laphroaig: 14 November 1994 | Current position: Distillery manager

John Campbell is an Ileach, by birth and heart. Twelve years after he joined the company as a warehouseman, he was appointed distillery manager. John comes from a family of farmers and fishermen. He cares deeply about the community on the island and Scotch whisky as a whole. 'My job as a distillery manager is broad: strategy, planning, operations, execution of these plans and team organisation.'

Since Robert Hicks' retirement in 2012, the Cairdeas cask selection is John's task. A team chosen from management and the warehouse assists him. 'I like to engage people with good noses and opinions. I know my abilities and limitations in choosing casks, so I will use others' noses to help.' John listens to his employees and tends to implement improvements they suggest. 'The distillery is no longer reliant on one person; the responsibilities are spread throughout the team. It renders more flexibility on site.' The main changes he underlines since he took up his position as the manager are to do with cutting waste time. It led to an increase of production that was instigated by 'Laphroaig's people, not by corporate demand higher up in the command chain'.

'We are mainly using barrels shipped straight from the US, not rebuilding them anymore into hoggies. I am very happy that we can use the casks just as they are. There is some minor coopering on site, but that is mostly repairs'. There is still room for experiments. 'We are filling small amounts of European oak casks, maybe 20 per year.' 66% of all production is maturing on site. In 2003 a special batch was distilled. 'We were trying to replicate the style from 100 years ago, only used the small stills, only malt from our own floor maltings, solely ex-bourbon barrels, and maturation in warehouse 1. Now it is available as the Cairdeas 2015, to celebrate the bicentenary.'

John travels four to five weeks in the year. 'I enjoy the ambassadorial work but I also enjoy my work at the distillery. I think it is very important to create a working environment where people are self-motivated.' The takeover by Suntory of Laphroaig's parent company Beam Global has not seen any major changes in leadership. Bowmore has become a sister distillery. 'Who knows, we might benefit from exchanging knowledge between the two of us in the near future.'

Laphroaig's 10-year-old remains John's favourite among the core expressions. 'I am not alone in that appreciation. There is a German guy who loves it so much that he had the barcode of Laphroaig 10 tattooed on his neck!'

# Vicky Stevens

Joined Laphroaig: 7 May 2008 | Current position: Manager Visitor Centre

Vicky Stevens was not born on Islay but on a farm near Garmouth in Speyside. The fields were fertilised with pot ale from Chivas Brothers. 'We had the greenest grass around'. She visited her first distillery when she was eight years old. It was a school trip to The Macallan. She attended high school in Fochabers and worked part time at Baxter's. 'They had a whisky shelf then, not a shop as they have nowadays.' When customers asked her for advice about whisky, she usually chose the shape of the bottle. 'I had a preference for Cardhu and Dimple.' In the late 1990s she worked for the owner of Orton Estate who ran a hedge fund of £ 3 billion in assets worldwide. Later she briefly worked for the Moray Council, but was already looking for another challenge.

'When I saw an ad for someone to manage the visitor centre at Laphroaig, I thought immediately that it was a fine opportunity to combine my business and finance knowledge with my customer service background.' She remembers her interview vividly. 'I was told that I would have to give a presentation of the 10-year-old, the 10-year-old cask strength, the 15-year-old and the Quarter Cask to a couple of directors. My prep was receiving a box with the four bottles on my doorstep – that's it, no guidance, and no tasting notes.' She combines her current job with being a brand ambassador, supporting sales and marketing. She writes tasting notes and helps choosing casks. Her favourite part is choosing new whisky expressions. And she loves the Friends of Laphroaig.

'I have never seen a program as interactive and honest as FoL. There are many available, but our following is tremendous. Last year we had over 72 different nationalities. It takes time to entertain them, but it's always worth it. One time a group of Israeli girls came running up the driveway, dragging their suitcases behind them. They were beyond closing time and I could not accommodate them. They went into tears, whereupon David Livingstone showed them around. Apparently they came over only to see their plot, then left the island again early the next morning.'

Robert Hicks greatly inspired her. 'He gave me confidence and huge energy.' So does a close relative. 'My granddad Shaw, my dad's dad, I would love to have a dram with him. My great-great-great granddad was clan chief of the Camerons of Lochiel. That's why I named my second daughter after my granddad.' She likes to have a whisky with friends. How she enjoys it depends upon what she is tasting, what is best suited for the circumstances: 'Sometimes I take it neat, sometimes with water, with food, or in a cocktail.'

Vicky realises that working at a distillery or in the whisky industry makes you feel very privileged to be part of that community. 'I meet other people from other brands, and there is no real animosity or rivalry, globally. The people working at the distillery are an extension of your family. Here I am, not from Islay. I started working here and the warehouse team immediately made fun of me, so I knew I would be accepted. That's when it all began, my love affair with Laphroaig!'

# David Livingstone

Joined Laphroaig: 2 October 2002 | Current position: Assistant Manager

David Livingstone was born and bred in Port Ellen, just down the road from Laphroaig where his father and grandfather worked in the past. David originally came on a temporary one-year-contract to work in the maltings. His contract was extended and he moved on to warehousing the next year, followed by four years of mashing and distilling. With hands-on experience in the different parts of the distillery, it was only logical that he ended up where he is now. 'When Beam took over and John was put in charge, I applied for his old job as Assistant Manager and have been fulfilling that role ever since.'

David really knows what is going on and he is a reliable source when it comes to finding out what has changed since we published the Legend of Laphroaig. 'We are producing record levels now. We've grown staff-wise. Everyone had to adapt and change. The visitor centre has snowballed with new people; there are almost 10 employed there now'.

According to David each day on the site is different. 'Arrive in the morning and the day can change in a second. You have to make as good a product as you can. Efficiency improved over the last seven years. When you look at things and break them down, there is a lot of scope to change the way you work.'

David is really proud of the place and his colleagues. 'More and more people come here and connect via Facebook. We've got the Friends but it is the family at Laphroaig that makes them. Shift operators make lifelong friendships with visitors. The last person who left employment wanted to come back but we had no vacancy.' John Campbell has been a great inspiration to him. 'He is always pointing you in the right direction and letting you go to find out yourself, to develop your own way of working and thinking.'

David is not a big drinker, but when he enjoys a dram he prefers to do that with a Friend of Laphroaig. 'The 18-year-old is my personal favourite, straight, not diluted. I do like bourbon, too.' He suddenly remembers an interesting event, some five years ago. 'I was all alone at the distillery and the phone rang. I picked it up and on the other side someone announced himself as Sean Connery, phoning from the Bahamas to thank us for a present that was sent to him. A bottle of 40-year-old Laphroaig. He wanted to talk to John, who was away on a business trip. I thought someone was playing a prank on me and asked all kinds of questions to check if it really was him. Well, eh, to cut a long story short, John phoned him back later…'

Guess with whom David would love to have a special dram of the 30-year-old, which he keeps at home behind lock and key? Laphroaig is made of legends like this.

# Barry MacAffer

Joined Laphroaig: 15 September 2011 | Current position: Maltman and management trainee

Barry MacAffer was raised in Ardbeg and Port Ellen, where he moved at age eight. He has had an interesting career to date. After finishing high school he went into the Merchant Navy for two years. A short stint on a fishing boat was followed by travelling around for one year. Barry ended up living and working in Glasgow as a dental technician. However, he wanted to come back to Islay and lives in Port Ellen with his girlfriend, who is a teacher at Port Ellen Primary.

That Islay, and Laphroaig, tugged on him to come back, may come as no surprise when looking at one of his relatives. Barry's great aunt was Rachel McAffer, the trusted secretary of Ian Hunter. His father was the child of Rachel's brother who also worked at Laphroaig and was even born at the distillery. His aunt Christine still has diaries from Rachel and her brother when they lived and worked at Laphroaig, pre-WWII. By the way Rachel preferred to leave the extra "a" out of MacAffer, but the rest of the family leaves it in.

He works in an eight-hour shift: 'There are four in the maltings team. Three work round the clock and one person comes in only 8am to 1pm. There is also a spare man on site to fill in where needed. Sometimes they do a 12 hour shift if someone needs time off.' The sea breeze might have an influence on the drying malt. The smell reminds him of Christmas dinner – fresh, malty. 'There is a hot air shaft from the kiln that blows the unpeated air in the malt floors in the winter if needed. It can raise the ambient temperature. This was added in the 2012 shut down period.' Christmas shutdown is about two weeks, the summer shutdown about three weeks.

'The malt is about 14-16 hours drying in the peated heat from the kiln, about 20 hours drying in the non-peated heat. After the first 10 hours, the malt is turned over in the kiln. You can tell the temperature difference just by going in the kiln and coming out and then know when to do the turn over.'

The malt men also tend the fires in the kiln. 'The more breeze, the more the draw in the kiln and more peat is needed to keep the flames down. There is also a fan in the pagoda to help with the draw. On a calm day, the kiln doors may need to be open. Opening or shutting the back door of the kiln area is the most important way to regulate the draw.'

Barry's eloquence is evident when he tells about his job. So is his enthusiasm and dedication. John Campbell must consider him 'high potential'. Since April 2014 Barry has been covering for David Livingstone as assistant manager on an as-needed basis.

# Arthur Holyoake

Joined Laphroaig: 12 August 2002 | Current position: Maltman

Arthur is a born Ileach and began working in the whisky industry in 1971. His first job was on the floor maltings at Lagavulin. 'I remember the Malt Mill distillery was still there, but not operating anymore'. Two years later Arthur moved to Port Ellen. 'At the time Duncan Brown was the head maltster. He taught me everything. My own father died at a young age, and Duncan naturally filled that void'. Between 1982 and 1983 Arthur worked as a distiller at Port Ellen until this distillery was closed. He went back to the maltings and would eventually take over Duncan Brown's job in 1993 – a position he held until he moved to Laphroaig. 'The company wanted me to stay in another position, but I could do no more to take Port Ellen further, so I applied for a job next door.'

He loves being a maltman and has seen many changes over the last 40 years. 'Until we had a moisture meter, which indicates that germination has to be stopped at 42%, we had manual ways to decide when to start kilning. For instance you would rub a grain between your thumb and finger or against a pole to see its character. The length of the spire is also an indicator. It should be  of the length of the grain.' He mentions another interesting fact: 'You must always be aware of water sensitive barley, which can soak up too much water if added all at once.  Thus you add the water slowly, over time, say 3 hours.  Port Ellen normally notifies us if the barley is water-sensitive.' Prior to the 1960s, barley would be tested on site in beakers for water sensitivity. 'We are now looking for 45% moisture content from the steeps and take samples after each airing.  Typically it is 30%, then the first air rest; 40%, then the second air rest; 45% and a third air rest.  Water sensitive barley will only go to 28% before its first air rest.'

Laying malt on the floor was originally called couching, but today the term casting is in use. 'There is a sweet, apply smell from a newly cast floor', Arthur enthusiastically points out. The biggest change in the maltings he witnessed during his career was the switch from manual to mechanical operation. 'We could suddenly control the heat and moisture far better.' 'We get between 35 and 65 ppm from our own floors. Port Ellen maltings delivers 35-45 ppm. Both malts are very different and we mix them before milling and mashing.'

Another change that had a big impact is the health and safety regulations. 'It's greatly improved for the employees.  I recall when men moving the barley would have strings tied around their trouser legs to prevent vermin from crawling up inside them. Or when men in the kiln just had a hankie over their noses when turning the malt by hand. Some of the guys used to roast rabbit and potatoes in the kiln fire, which is unthinkable now with all those regulations.'

Arthur is a great storyteller and an amateur author. Currently he is writing a piece for the whisky centennial, ensuring the product he creates maintains the standard of the generations before him. He is the one to do it. After all, his nickname is The Malt Legend. His other big passion is golf. He is the only person to have won the Kildalton Golf Tournament five times!

# William 'Windy' Campbell

Joined Laphroaig: 16 April 1979 | Current positions: Brewer/distiller, alternating

Born in Glasgow, Windy was only three weeks old when his parents moved to Islay because his father got a job at the Port Ellen maltings. Spirit runs in the family.

A former builder, Windy began at Laphroaig as a cooper, followed by jobs in the warehouse and the filling store. In 1988 he switched to the mash house and for the last 17 years he has combined mashing, brewing and distilling. Windy remembers the Big Still being replaced. 'The old one was worn out completely. It was 1 mm thin in places, proved by an ultra- sound test. It started to bend in at the height of your knees when you looked into it.'

Windy is the one to ask how all stills work together. 'Well, the #1 wash still fills the #2 spirit still; the #2 wash still fills the # 3 spirit still and the #3 wash still fills the #4 spirit still. The #1 spirit still, the Big One, is filled as and when the feints receiver gets full enough. It is not paired with a wash still.'

A logbook and a calendar are used to keep track of things that need to be repaired or replaced. 'We often see it coming and work our way around it, doing preventive maintenance with parts from other machines.'

He takes his job seriously but likes to joke, too. The morning we were to interview him, there was something wrong with the mash tun. He actually had to get into it first, to clean it and check out the issue. When he came out, there was a tour on, so the participants were a bit surprised to see his head pop out. He asked them 'Is this Australia?' much to everyone's amusement.

Windy alternates shifts with his cousin Billy Johnston, whose surname is not unknown to Laphroaig. 'I'm not sure if I can trace back my ancestry to founder Donald, but I'd like to think it is the case.'

# Billy Johnston

Joined Laphroaig: 1 June 1989 | Current positions: Brewer/distiller, alternating

According to Billy the flavour of the spirit coming from the Big Still is only slightly different from that of the small stills. 'It evens out in the filling room, where the spirit of all four stills is blended anyway'.

He explains a couple of things about running the stills. 'The wash charger is in the boiler house, and can hold just over 2 washbacks, close to 100,000 litres. In the still house we have an intermediate spirit receiver with a capacity to hold 33,000 litres of spirit. The warehouse men will let us know how much to pump over to their receivers. They have two with a capacity of 36,000 litres in each. Our feints receiver sits behind the wash condensers and can hold approximately 50,000 litres.'

'The small spirit stills take about five hours to run. 10 minutes to get the still running, then 45 minutes foreshots, two hours and fifteen minutes of spirit [middle cut, 900 litres] and two hours of feints. The spirit is stored in the stillhouse, then pumped to the filling store. There will be about 6,000 litres of pot ale left from a wash still and about 2,000 litres of spent lees from the spirit still. There is a heat exchanger that removes the heat from these for heating the next round. '

'We've been using touch screens for the charging and discharging of the stills for a while and since Christmas 2013 the input of steam has been automated. It is all part of One Beam Way – a method using time and energy as efficiently as possible.'

Billy's father used to work at Laphroaig and had a collection of old Laphroaig bottles. Billy started to sell these bottles via eBay. He shares his sense of humour with his cousin Windy. This cordial member of the Johnston clan also happens to be a talented amateur photographer and a proud grandfather.

# James McGregor
Joined Laphroaig: 20 October 1975 | Current position: Warehouseman

Born in Bowmore, with a father who used to be an engineer at Laphroaig; one daughter studying to get into the whisky industry after an internship at Ardbeg and another working at the Harbour Inn, you can say with certainty he is anchored on Islay. 'There are six women in my life. That's why I'm so bald. I have three more daughters and my wife, who used to work for the police.' Furthermore he has been enjoying 40 years of employment at Laphroaig in the year the distillery celebrates its bicentenary. James started the same week when Denis Nicol became distillery manager. 'He was a good man, concerned with the community, raised money for a swimming pool. And he used to do all the lab stuff himself'.

He remembers his former bosses well. 'Murdo Reed was straight to the point. If he didn't know something, he would ask.' Colin Ross came from Ben Nevis and would eventually go back there. 'He always used to say, "that's not how we did it up in the Ben."' The sturdy Ileach also has a good description of Iain Henderson: 'He didn't hold a grudge. He might tell you off, but then it was over, never brought it up again.' About Robin Shields, who was only distillery manager at Laphroaig for a short time, he recalls: 'He was a nice man, a brewer.'

James started as a warehouseman, moved to the tun room, then to drying draff, followed by a stint at the maltings, then to the still house and back to the warehouses. 'Each new boss wanted some things different'. Today the warehouse crew consists of four men. 'Usually it's one man on filling the tanker and three men working on loading/unloading/filling barrels. Some barrels and some tankers are going to customers'. All men are working 4.5 days a week. With the increase in production they are working hard to keep up. 'Warehouses 1, 8 and 9 are the only places with space for sherry butts. There are some hoggies in 9 and 10A. The angel's share is pretty consistent at 2%, no real hot spots in the warehouses. No. 1 warehouse is the best; stone built, close to the sea.' Laphroaig's warehousing on the mainland is in Westthorn, Glasgow. 'It is close to the Celtic football pitch. I remember once some barrels supposedly floated away in a Glasgow flood.'

He knows the distillery and its history well. Pointing at the metal racks in warehouse No. 8 he remarks: 'They've been around for a while. They used to hold petrol barrels in World War II.' On the upper floors of Warehouse 1: 'There are still blackout smudges on the windows.' He also has a historical explanation for the lines painted on the floor of the barley loft. 'That's were the soldiers used to camp out during the war.'

Friends of Laphroaig impact all employees of the distillery. James for instance, made some Swedish friends and went to visit them in the summer of 2014. The longest-serving employee of Laphroaig expects to stay around until his retirement. He might even celebrate his 50th anniversary of working at the distillery. When asked which expression of Laphroaig he'd like to share with his friends, the answer is unequivocal: 'Triple Wood'.

# Emma Boyle

Joined Laphroaig: 9 May 2005 | Current position: Assistant Visitor Centre Manager

Emma is from Port Ellen, from a large island family. She loves Islay. On her 19th birthday she walked up to the distillery for an interview – 'I had no driver's license yet' – and became one of the very first tour guides at Laphroaig. 'When we started we did two tours and in between we simply locked the door of the visitor centre. Every day the two were fully booked, so we had to come up with expansion plans. It went gradually but today we have five standard tours and two special ones, themed to water and warehouses.' Over time she started to do ambassadorial work and came up with new ideas for the shop and the visitor centre. 'We sell a lot of cheese with Laphroaig in it now. The Glencairn tasting glass is a popular item as well.

Emma is also heavily involved in the communication with the Friends of Laphroaig (FOL) and answers many letters and requests. She remembers one of the main reasons that FOL was started. 'Laphroaig had a lot of land to protect the water source and wanted to use that land. Due to drainage issues, nothing permanent can be built there.' But you can surely give away lifetime leases to square feet of it! You can't take it home either. 'We had a Japanese Friend who went into the fields and cut out his plot. He came back with it to the visitor centre and wanted to pack it and take it home. Well, he probably didn't make it through airport security with it', Emma laughs.

She is also involved in local activities and organises a yearly day for local businesses and encourages them to take a tour, a tasting and inform their own customers. 'Many locals return to buy the cheese.' Emma cares for the community. 'I have three horses. One of them is a little pony and I teach children to ride.' She is a big animal lover anyway and had hamsters, rabbits, cats and dogs as a child, notwithstanding the fact that her mother didn't like the critters at all. 'We had many stray cats hanging around. One day I put an old creel in the garden with a piece of meat, caught a cat and hid him in the shed for while. Mum didn't appreciate that.'

Does she have any plans to leave Islay? 'Not really. I love my job with Laphroaig. You don't feel you are living on an island. I also travel regularly for the company and have been to Ireland, Sweden and Edinburgh.' Islay has changed in the last 20 years. 'Without tourism that would not have happened. We had 12,000 visitors annually at Laphroaig when I started 10 years ago. Now that number has tripled.' The island co-developed with that growth. 'Our merchandise grew, the flights became more affordable, more ferries arrive daily. There are more B&B's, hotels and restaurants. Feis Ile also is very important to Islay. There are more job opportunities for younger people. And the community as a whole benefits from that.'

Her first Laphroaig was the much-lauded 15-year-old, which made a comeback recently. Emma's father unfortunately died when she was still young. 'My favourite dram would be one I could share with him.'

# Bryony Boyd

Joined Laphroaig: 4 January 2011 | Current position: Visitor Centre Host and Tour Guide

Bryony grew up at Lord Margadale's Estate where her father was appointed forester when she was two years old. 'My mother arrived to a 16-room house', she fondly remembers.

After primary school in Bridgend and high school in Bowmore she took a job as her father's secretary and got to know the estate well. A genuine love for nature was one of the results. In following years she pursued various administrative jobs on the island, until she responded to an ad from Laphroaig in the Ileach, the local newspaper. 'My job interview was in October. The sun was going down like a red ball behind the Oa. I thought, how I would love working beside the sea.'

Bryony got interested in the way the staff was trained. She was impressed with the quality and support encountered. With the team growing bigger, the programs on offer had to be developed. More visitors had to be accommodated. It meant lots of variety in her daily work routine. 'It didn't take too long to get settled and feeling comfortable in my new position. Today I enjoy meeting people from everywhere. I am really content in my wee Islay-bubble!'

The Water to Whisky Tour is one of her favourites to execute. It takes 4.5 hours with a small group of no more than eight people. This tour is on offer from March till September. 'When you spend half a day with a group, you get to know them a little.'

When Bryony takes visitors to the peat bog, she shows them how to cut the peat and hands over the equipment to each one of them. After their attempts, which differ from successful to disastrous, she shares a dram on Machrie Moor with them, before returning to the distillery. 'The Friends of Laphroaig love to come and visit their plot. It makes a connection with the heart. After all, it is quite an effort for a Chinese or Japanese visitor to get to Islay.'

Pacing to find the plots is not done anymore. GPS trackers are now available which makes it a lot easier. Not for everybody, though. One time three Greek military men stationed in Brussels, came down, looking for their plots, but couldn't find them. 'We had a good banter and I went back with them the next morning, showing them the exact spot' she laughs.

Bryony, a warm-hearted woman, can tell lots of stories about Friends and their particular behaviour. She also receives presents from them. 'One of your fellow countrymen once gave me a pair of clogs!' She enjoys a dram herself and takes a particular liking to the 18-year-old. 'That's the whisky I would share with my Granny or maybe my father. They've had a big influence on my life.'

# Nigel MacTaggart

Joined Laphroaig: 6 February 1989 I Current position: Maintenance Technician

If someone knows all the nuts and bolts of the distillery, it must be Nigel MacTaggart, another true Ileach at Laphroaig. He left school at 16 and went into engineering at Abercrombie in Alloa, the maintenance department of DCL, (today's Diageo). For a decade he worked at distilleries all over the UK. In 1987 he decided to return to Islay and applied for a job at Bowmore. A year later he switched to Laphroaig, shortly before the distillery was acquired by Allied. 'And I've been here ever since!' His department shrank over the years. 'When I started we had one engineer, a full time electrician and a chief engineer. Now it's only me'. Nigel is on call 24/7 for 46 weeks out of the year and has to be present during the shut downs, when most maintenance takes place. When he is on holiday, one of Diageo's maintenance men functions as a back up.

The big changes over the years were in automation. 'A lot of money has been invested and I had to learn all that new stuff. Years ago it was mostly manual labour and physically more demanding than now.' In theory the mashing and distilling process can be monitored from up in Aberdeenshire. 'They simply go to their lap top and run an analysis if there's a problem.' When something breaks down it is easier to get new components. 'I have a company laptop and just order spare parts via the internet.' It used to take much longer, when orders had to be placed and delivered via Glasgow. 'Well, on a rock in the Atlantic, parts delivery can be a bit slow', he grins.

Nigel's knowhow is imperative. when planning. 'It influences the equipment, always. We sit down and discuss what is involved, maintenance-wise, and usually draw up 18 months plans to work from.' When asked about recent changes at the distillery, Nigel easily pipes up with some examples. 'The boiler was replaced after 30 years of service. We went from 100 psi to 150 psi. Now the oil usage is much lower and more efficient. By increasing the pump size for the heat exchangers we could crank up production without increasing capacity by ways of extra wash backs or stills. This relatively inexpensive modification took us from 2.1 to 3.2 million litres annually.'

Nigel has a son who is a joiner and carpenter on Islay. His daughter is a musician who plays tin whistle, accordion and guitar. She acquired her degree in Glasgow and is a music teacher. Nigel's parents were Gaelic speakers, but he does not practise it himself. 'At primary school one of the old guys asked my friend where his Gaelic was. He said, I took it out of my mouth and threw it in the Sound!'

He's been around long enough to have witnessed both Royal visits of HRH Prince Charles. 'The 1994 was a huge disappointment regarding press attention. They were focused on the plane crash and not on Laphroaig. The 2008 visit was a very enjoyable one, with Camilla present, too. 'The 30-year-old, is his favourite Laphroaig: 'I would immediately share with my father'. Whisky runs in their family – MacTaggart Senior spent his working life as a brewer at Caol Ila Distillery.

# Caroline Morris

Joined Laphroaig: 19 March 1990 | Current position: Company Secretary and Administrator

Caroline Morris was only a week old when she moved to Islay. 'My grandparents came from London to the Oa to farm. My father inherited the land and later sold part of it to the RSPB, but still owns several houses there. My mother is from Glasgow, originally, but settled well on Islay.' Caroline is one out of ten people that have been working at Laphroaig for more than a quarter century. 'Employees did not change much, up until the last six or seven years, when we started to recruit new people.' Her job has changed over the years. 'At first I had to register barrels going out, as well as tankers, but that is done centrally now. Back then we had no real visitor centre, but I did the occasional distillery tour. I loved the people and it did build my confidence. I learned a lot about the whisky making process.' She sure knows what's all happening at the distillery.

Caroline  gets all kinds of calls and follows up accordingly. 'A pensioner ordered a six bottle case of 10-year-old every two weeks. Then his doctor told him to stop drinking. Then his blood pressure seriously rose. Well, said the doctor in response, better continue then.' When a depressed woman phoned after having enjoyed a bit too much Laphroaig, Caroline would listen patiently, a sort of social worker, with great empathy. No wonder she deals with the follow up of special sensitive requests from Friends of Laphroaig (FOL). 'When her husband passed away, a widow rang us up and asked for a plaque on his plot. Barry, Jenny and I took it there, made a photograph and sent it to her. She wired some money and requested a rosebush on the plot, but that would not survive in the moors. So we planted it in front of the visitor centre, where it still can be found.'

As various other members of Laphroaig's staff, Caroline is involved in projects that benefit the community on Islay. 'We have the plastic dog in the visitor centre, where people can donate money for the Guide Dog Association.  We auction bottles online and support local initiatives with the proceeds. Recently we raised £5,000 towards a heating system for the Islay Museum.' Another recipient is Port Ellen Primary School, where Caroline went herself when a child.

Both Royal visits, in 1994 and 2008 respectively, made a great impression on her. 'In 1994 we heard on the news about the accident with the plane. When HRH showed up he was very down to earth and easy to speak to. I recall being very nervous. In 2008 I was picked out to ask Camilla a question. HRH recognised me and said: 'We did meet the last time'.' She also vividly remembers what her colleagues were doing at the time. 'Eddy, David, James and Nigel were in kilt, playing drums with the pipe band. And John spoke to Prince Charles in Warehouse No. 1, sharing a dram with him.' When asked with whom Caroline would prefer to do such a thing, she promptly answers: With Cliff Richard… or my dad!'

It's all whisky in her family anyway. Her husband has been working at Bunnahabhain distillery for nearly 20 years and is the son of legendary warehouseman Eddie Morris.

# Eddie Morris
28 December 1946 | Retired from Laphroaig as of 2012

Born a Londoner, Eddie Morris has been living most of his life on Islay. He grew up at Laphroaig distillery since his father, a former English RAF man stationed on Islay, met his mother on the island and consequently worked at Laphroaig's warehouses for more than 30 years. At the age of 15, Eddie started his working career at Ardenistle Farm (belonging to Laphroaig) also taking care of the nursery, which supplied the whole island with flowers. It was the time of Bessie Williamson, when workers had free housing and a free load of coal for heating, delivered by horse cart every month. When the farm was discontinued in 1963, Eddie went to work for Port Ellen Distillery. When its distilling operations were terminated in 1983, he returned to his former stomping grounds.

'I remember I was the mash man at Port Ellen and preferred an eight to five job. Murdo Reed was the manager when I applied at Laphroaig to come back. Straight as a dye, he went by the book, a fair man.' Eddie gives an example: 'At the time I was in the fire brigade as a volunteer. So I asked Mr Reed what to do when my pager went off. He said, "Just wait till it happens."' Eddie was given the same job as his father – warehouseman.

'It was the times that I worked with Gordon McKechnie, David Adams and Hamish Campbell, for whom I cut the grass when I was a boy. These guys taught me the ropes.' Eddie enjoyed being back at Laphroaig: 'It was a nice and relaxing job before the extensive health and safety regulations were put in place. Then it became more difficult, but the guys were still good to work with.'

When prompted about the times with Bessie, he recalls: 'I used to drive Bessie & Mr Wishart around in their car. I did not care much for him but I can honestly say that Bessie Williamson was the nicest woman I've met in my life.' Eddie illustrates her kindness with a couple of anecdotes; 'I remember a party once at Halloween. Sixteen kids were invited to go up her house. There was a big basin of water and the kids had to dive for candy. At Christmas Bessie would host a party for the kids, also those at Lagavulin. I think there were 40 or 50 of them and she paid for all of it.' The kind lady distiller donated to various causes. 'She put a lot of money in things like playing fields for football, golf and such. All for the good of the community.' Bessie was also involved with the Woman Royal Institute and would arrange for movies on the island. 'She would send Dougie MacNeil and I to Church Hall or Laphroaig Hall and we operated the projector.'

Eddie tells his stories with some kind of mild satisfaction in his voice and changes the subject: 'When I came back in 1983 I was the spare guy, and was used everywhere, but I loved the warehouse. I was more interested in filling the barrels than producing the whisky.' Remarkably enough for a warehouseman who has dealt with millions of liters of maturing whisky, Eddy doesn't drink a single drop. 'My father didn't either', he gently concludes.

# Denis Nicol
Retired | Managed Laphroaig between 1974 and 1980

Born on 6 January 1942 in Glasgow, Denis Nicol moved to Wigtown as a baby and would eventually receive a degree in Pure Science at Glasgow University. After three months of teaching he responded to an ad in the *Glasgow Herald* and joined Canadian owned Hiram Walker at their Dumbarton offices as a chemist until 1970. At that point, 'I wanted to become a distillery manager'. Tormore had a vacancy and Denis moved to the Highlands. 'Quite a change of scenery, I recall the winters were very fierce. One time the effluent plant froze solid.'

As a university student he didn't particularly care for whisky, but had tasted Laphroaig and thought it was something special. 'I did research at Hiram Walker on phenols, comparing Highland to Islay peat, looking at the phenol spectrum. I had collected lots of analytical data on phenols. There was one that wiped out your sense of smell for two days. I was involved in preparing a complete phenol spectrum of Laphroaig malt whisky resulting in a detailed scientific paper of the role of peat in Laphroaig's flavour spectrum.'

In 1974 he saw Laphroaig for the first time. 'It was the epitome of a West Highland distillery. It embodied everything you had to know about making whisky. It had a peat moss. Measurements that were unbeknownst to me: they were using chains and furlongs. It was medieval, like stepping back in time. They cut the peat by hand, damaging the peat moss much less than with an extruder.'

Denis was responsible for two legendary vintage bottlings, loved by many Laphroaig fans: the 1976 and the 1977. According to him the whisky was made very differently from how it is made today. 'The 80 hour fermentation enables *Lactobacillus* bacteria to become established, producing a more mellow, less harsh new product. So it's always a balance between good whisky and good yields.' For his taste, Laphroaig is too young at 10. 'I'd go for the 15-year-old immediately. Five years make a huge difference. The cask influence is greater, so the peatiness is less at 15.'

Talking about casks: 'The cooper at Long John was in charge of cask selection. Bourbon casks originally came in staves. You could make hoggies out of them or reconstruct as they were. Someone asked, "Why are we paying the coopers all that money?". So then the casks came over already put together. Maybe 1 in 100 leaked. The leakers were a risk – but HMRC didn't charge for those. The casks were coming over from George Dickel.'

Denis has fond memories about his time at Laphroaig and on Islay. A good friend, Angie Mor McAffer had been to see Doctor Archie G. MacKinnon, a native Gaelic speaker and local GP who enjoyed a good dram. Angus came to see Denis, having tried to pry money out of Archie to start an undertaker's business. Angus wanted £200 out of Denis for this ploy. He remarked that between 'The Doctor, the Distiller and himself he could set up a good business'. Unfortunately, suspecting that he might have been a bit 'under the weather', Denis chased him away. Angie Mor McAffer went on to establish an undertaker's business driving a Mercedes. Eventually his son took over the business.

'I also remember Rachel McAffer well. Lovely lady, a stalwart. She fell out one time with Iain McLean, the warehouse man. They'd never spoken to each other since Iain swept the chimneys in the office without telling the people there he was going to do this. The whole place was covered in soot, a huge mess. This happened in 1937. Whitbread invited them in 1977 for a long service celebration. They were forced to break their silence after 40 years!'

'One time two chemists from the government laboratory visited, both holding a PhD. I offered them a dram. They wanted to know if this was ok with Her Majesty's Customs & Excises. A lot of booha, but they did accept the drink, and after, one of them said: 'Well, there is Laphroaig and the Rest.' The rest for Denis, when he left Laphroaig, meant working as a project scientist at Western Labs (part of then owner Whitbread too). 'All research. Strange things. Like trying to capture the angels' share. Completely blocking off a warehouse and using an activated carbon column to extract the air from the warehouse. Didn't work. Or capturing ethanol from the fermentation gas stream in a grain distillery. It was all piped through a water column. That actually worked.'

A scientist at heart, Denis would end up in charge of all Allied Domecq laboratories and took a seat on the Distillation Committee of the Pentlands Scotch Whisky Research Institute. He officially retired in 1996 but was hired as a consultant for a rum distillery in Guyana for a year, then wrote a series of scientific articles and even ended up drinking 'firewater in a wee bothy in the Himalayas.' For a good dram he does not have to travel very far. 'I like sharing a dram with Captain Lamont Ross who lives next door. He has a good supply of malt whiskies. Originally from Skye, as a deep sea ship's captain, there is hardly a corner of the world unknown to him. His children maintain his stocks.'

Denis still feels deeply about Islay and the Ileachs. When the time comes, he wishes his ashes to be scattered on Islay's highest hill, Ben Bheigir.

# Murdo Reed

Retired | Managed Laphroaig between 1980 and 1987

Although born in Forfar on 4 March 1944 and having lived in Tanzania as a young boy, Murdo considers Aberdeenshire his home, where he lived from age seven until his late 20s. Ever since his father had died in Tanzania he wanted to support his mother and siblings. So, at the age of 16 he applied for a job with Teacher's and was taken on as an administrative worker in 1960 at their Ardmore distillery.

His official working days were Monday to Friday from 8 am till 5 pm, but he often came back to learn about distilling and would stay until midnight. Sometimes he would lend an extra hand in at sister distillery Glendronach. Over time Murdo would work in all departments and acquired a thorough knowledge about distillation. He would never participate in dramming, and eventually drank his first whisky when he was 29.

Despite his extensive hands-on knowledge, Murdo felt he lacked a theoretical management background. He took a two-year course at Aberdeen Tech, receiving his certificate from the Institute of Managers, and was appointed assistant to the Distillery Manager. Mind you, he managed to do this while working a more than eight-hours-a-day job.

When a vacancy came up at Laphroaig, Murdo, who was in for a new challenge, applied for the manager's position. Notwithstanding the fact that colleagues and friends advised him not to go because it was supposed to be rather rundown and...remote. Murdo approached it differently and thought the only way Laphroaig could go was up. He recalls: Laphroaig was in dire need of renovation.'

He saw the potential, but feared being on an island with not much of a support system from headquarters. That whole system would have to be built up. In hindsight he says: 'Whitbread and Long John turned out to be one of my best employers.' He sat down with John McDougall, who oversaw Glenugie, Laphroaig and Tormore at the time and discussed various plans for the distillery and salesstrategies. Together they painted a 5 to 10 year plan to get Laphroaig back in shape. 'It was clear to me the owners wanted to spend money on the distillery...the plan turned out to be a combination of brand vision and a vision of improving the distillery and that made me take the job'.

Apart from the maltings almost everything at Laphroaig would be changed during his seven year tenure, as can be read in detail in the previous chapter. Murdo was not very much involved in cask selection for bottling. 'I mainly worked with Robert Hicks and Denis Nicol on that matter, but being responsible for checking if the received casks were of a good quality.'

Murdoch lived in the Manager's house. His wife and daughter came in October of 1980 because his wife had wanted to stay with her mother for the first few months after she delivered. 'My daughter spent the first seven years of her life on Islay and has many happy memories from that time. Once she started walking, she would walk down the back hall from the house and visit Betty McAffer and John Calder in the office. She now is an oil operator and has a young son.'

When he took the Laphroaig job, Murdo had said that he didn't want to stay on the island forever. 'After five years, there was an industry downturn and it wasn't the right time to move around. Our sister distillery Tormore was getting a new by-product treatment plant, so I moved there in 1987'. He saw it as a promotion and moved to Grantown on Spey. 'Once the plant was running, it was one of my easiest jobs ever thanks to the team around me', he recalls.

Then Allied took over Whitbread. Murdo was on holiday but insisted he tell the employees of Tormore himself. The new owner scrapped many perks, including the free housing at Tormore. Staff could either pay rent, buy the house or move out. 'Most moved out. They asked me to stay but I saw limited chances within the new company structure and decided to leave altogether.'

In 1990 he moved to Glenmorangie and stayed on as manager until 1994. He more or less did what he had done at Laphroaig and modernised the distillery. He was not only responsible for introducing a fax machine but more importantly, a new still house. The latter would aptly be nicknamed 'the cathedral'. After a sabbatical he moved to nearby Invergordon where he held the position of Spirit Handling Manager until 2006, when he retired. 'I loved my job, but now my time is filled with golf, curling, walking and spending time with my grandson.'

Murdo has a fondness for the 15-year-old Laphroaig and prefers it with a drop of water. The amiable former distillery manager never took a sick day in his entire working career. His explanation is simple and straightforward: 'an active teenage life, a wee dram most nights and sheer good luck'.

# Colin Ross

Retired | Managed Laphroaig between 1987 and 1989

Colin Ross was born on 27 February 1948 in the hospital at Forres Morayshire and grew up in Elgin and Fochabers, where he attended high school. After his 5th year of higher education he took up the position as trainee Distillery Manager with Chivas Brothers in Keith, working in their general office, located in Strathisla Distillery.

'My first view of Laphroaig was in 1977 when Denis Nicol invited me over. He used to be my manager at Tormore before he went to Islay.' From that early visit he recalls: 'An engineer was giving some of the guys haircuts in a break room. About the same time I visited Glenugie. Both distilleries needed money spent and Laphroaig ended up receiving major investments. Glenugie was closed in 1983.'

Colin went from Tormore to Ben Nevis and eventually moved to Islay during the summer shut-down of August 1987. 'It was a company decision. At first I didn't want to go. I was asked to move with the entire family. My father had recently passed away, my wife held a good job and the children were in high school. However, when headquarters challenged me with saying "You are not wanting to go to Laphroaig as you are not capable of holding that position." I could only but agree to go just to prove to them that I could do the job.' So Colin went with the explicit task of increasing production, without actually knowing what that would do to the spirit. 'The improvements Murdo Reed had put in place cost a lot of money. I had a more modest budget.' Headquarters insisted on an extra intermediate spirit receiver. 'We could now increase the production of the spirit before being casked. HQ then requested that we ship out the new spirit in tankers and then taken to the mainland, so we started to fill the tankers with a hose, directly from the filling store. The whisky would then be transported to Westthorn, Glasgow, to mature in the warehouses there.'

Colin remembers an interesting story connected to that event. 'Mind you, when I was at Laphroaig there was no resident officer of H.M. Customs & Excise anymore. We had a Mr Mike Stringer, living in a rented cottage in Port Ellen. He would take care of duties at various distilleries.' The day Colin first used the tankers and the hose, Revenue Assistant Betty Campbell arrived unannounced at the scene and demanded to know what was happening. He answered innocently, 'What does it look like? We're loading this tanker with new make Laphroaig spirit for shipment to Glasgow as instructed by my superiors there.' Betty about turned and drove off site and we just carried on loading the tanker, which then went off on the next ferry for the mainland. I thought, good job, well done, and it cost the company little more than a bit of food grade hose. About 4:30 p.m., a really angry Mike Stringer arrived on site asking what did I think I was doing, and again, in all innocence, I told him what we had done. It was only when he said "but you do not have permission for such operations" that I realised the gravity of the situation. Apparently, as this had never been done before, I should have been in contact with H.M. C&E to request their permission and then waited until this was granted before we had embarked on such an exercise. I am sure that we were in the habit of disgorging mature whisky from casks and shipping that in bulk to the mainland so I never thought that permission had to be sought before proceeding with the shipment of new spirit in this way. Mike Stringer had been out at sea on the Customs rib inflatable carrying out a routine drugs exercise when Betty Campbell had contacted him and was unable to do anything about what we were doing at the time but had stated that had he been on the island rather than out at sea he would have stopped the operation altogether. Up until that time I had a very good relationship with Mike but I have to say that he was not happy with me after that, as I am sure that he would have been in trouble with his superiors. This must have been a very serious breach of the regulations.'

When the C&E Officers finally moved to the mainland and would occasionally visit Islay for periodical inspections, Colin knew to be prepared. 'Whenever Customs & Excise sent over their 'rummage squad' to inspect the distilleries on the island, the staff at MacBrayne's office would ring ahead to inform their Islay Office that they were on their way and then the 'bush telegraph' took over and alerted all distilleries beforehand.'

On another occasion Colin had to deal with a strike. Islay is very vulnerable in such a case and relatively minor happenings on the mainland can have far stretching consequences for the distilleries on the island. 'We were using DCL distillers yeast, but due to a ferry strike could not get yeast onto the island. John Calder, an ex-Glasgow policeman who worked in administration and security at the Laphroaig offices, had a son-in-law with a fishing boat – problem solved.'

Sometimes Colin's function resembled that of a tour guide more than a distillery manager. He had to entertain people from all over the world, mostly trade associates. 'We sold a lot of Laphroaig in bulk to Nikka and Suntory at the time.' He describes a typical day:

'Check with Dr Jim Taylor, Assistant Distillery Manager
Jump in the bus (the Vomit Comet) and get visitors from airport
Take visitors for coffee
Guided tour through the distillery
Take to Bridgend for lunch
Drop at the Machrie for golf (non-golfers were given a tour around the island)
Check in at the distillery
Supper with guests
We sometimes did that 5-6 days a week, especially in the summer.'

When Whitbread sold Ben Nevis to Nikka in 1989, the Japanese asked Colin Ross to come back to 'The Ben'. He's been there ever since and celebrates 50 years in the whisky business in 2015.

# Iain Henderson

Retired | Managed Laphroaig between 1989 and 2002

Appropriately nicknamed Mr Laphroaig during his time at the distillery, Iain Henderson ran Laphroaig for 14 consecutive years, having been the longest serving in this post after Bessie Williamson sold the distillery to Long John.

Iain was born on 18 November 1937 and grew up in Edinburgh, where he lived throughout World War II and witnessed as a young boy the German attack known as the 'Forth Bridge Raid'. It made a lasting impression on him. His father, a wireless operator during the war, originally was a trained shoemaker and made shoes for the Queen. Only one pair came back. 'So my mother got to wear a pair of HM's shoes', he chuckles. From the tender age of 12 Iain would have various jobs and eventually went into an engineering apprenticeship. At age 19 he got a job at the Merchant Navy. Two years later he'd gone around the world a couple of times. Back then he was first acquainted with Laphroaig, in Australia, not knowing that many, many years later he would come to run the distillery and be one of the founding fathers of the Friends of Laphroaig. 'For a time I was running Ardbeg as well. One of my protégées was Michael Heads. He was a young lad at the time and asked if he could come and help, for free. That's how he got started, as a brewer. I trained and taught him.'

Eventually Mickey Heads was offered a job on Jura. 'We were sitting in the Port Askaig pub and he agonised over whether to leave Islay or not. He thought that he was letting me down. But I advised him to go and take that opportunity. Now he is back at Ardbeg, as the manager.' Co-incidentally Ardbeg and Laphroaig both celebrate their bicentenary in 2015. Iain is still in touch with his former protégée, who repaid the favour by advising the former's son on his professional career in Elgin.

During Iain's tenure Laphroaig bought back casks from independent bottlers, among which those whose contents ended up in the famous 30 and 40-year-old bottlings. 'It was the marketing department that made those decisions. I wrote the tasting notes for the 30-year-old, it was the only one I was involved with. The policy was that the 10 was the bread and butter. There wasn't a structure to promote the malts. That's where Jeremy Weatherhead from marketing really came into his own. They used to sometimes put the 15 out twice a year in a special tin with a big 15 on it.' The 10 has always been Iain's favourite. 'When I arrived at Laphroaig distillery I had not even heard about the 15.'

Not only Iain but also his wife Carol was very much involved with Laphroaig. 'She used to do the catering for big events, among which four weddings at the distillery. And we always had a dance in the summer, and a dance at Christmas time, and Carol catered it all!' When needed she also acted as tour guide *avant la lettre*.

The Hendersons are gone but not forgotten at Laphroaig. Caroline Morris refers to Iain's wife as Mrs. H to this day. 'We're still in touch and I keep telling her that she should get her boys off the island for a while. Let them see something of the world.'

When Iain turned 65, Suntory, long time customer of Laphroaig, took him to Tokyo for his birthday. He remembers it well. 'Christine Logan had come along and was dressed up as a geisha. And Michael Jackson was there, doing the presentations, telling the audience that I was now officially retired. We didn't recognise Christine, who, for the occasion, had made a cake in the shape of Laphroaig.' Suntory would organise no less than 10 farewell dinners for him, in a span of two weeks. Today their involvement with Laphroaig could not be greater. With the acquisition of Beam Global in 2014, they came to own the distillery.

Iain would have loved to stay on much longer but company regulations did not allow that. So he moved to Fife and went on, advising start-up distilleries, among which St George in Norfolk, and helping established ones, such as Edradour near Pitlochry.

He still misses Islay and its people dearly. 'It's the laid-back casualness, the relaxed attitude. It's that strip of water. Your boss can't come unannounced; the gals at the airport would have called me to say they were coming. We ran the distillery like a little family. We knew the little problems the guys had, we tried to help resolve them. I felt the guys there had some respect for you, when you were trying to do something to correct them or discipline them. We had some great fun!'.

# In the Bottle

## History

More than two centuries ago, when distilling in Scotland was still an artisan craft, legal or illegal, the prospective buyer had to bring his own container to either tap the liquid straight from the still or the cask. Glassware, being rather expensive at the time, would have been rare. More likely earthenware jugs were used, similar to the ones sold today as reminders of days gone by.

Fortunate whisky drinkers could afford to buy whole casks and have those delivered to their cellars at home. We can imagine that the whisky inside would then be measured into crystal decanters by a servant, taken upstairs to the library and poured into glasses for distinguished guests. Not much attention was paid to specific brands or identifiers from where the whisky came, more to the whisky broker from whom the cask was purchased or the distillery where it was made.

Only when glass bottles became more affordable, around the 1850s, the need to distinguish one bottle from the other became more apparent. One of the first, if not the first to present his name on the bottle as a brand, was John Dewar, somewhere in the 1870s. He did not do this by pasting a label on the front, but by having his signature blown into the glass. He switched to paper a mere 15 years later  - the oldest surviving bottle that carries his name on a paper label is from 1885.

It could have been another famous blended whisky that was the first to use labels. William Teacher and Sons, a long time sibling to Laphroaig, owns two bottles with fragments of what might have been the first label ever. The remains cannot be accurately dated but the bottles on which they are glued were identified as the type used in the 1860s.

The first labels to appear on bottles were mostly printed in black on a white background. Sometimes with one or two colours, on a paper already coloured to add another tint. Thanks to Alfred Barnard, who illustrated his tome The Whisky Distilleries of the United Kingdom with some examples of these labels, we know what they looked like in 1887, when the book was published.

At first the label was merely used as part of the packaging design and to create brand awareness. The majority didn't show any information regarding the alcoholic content or even the amount of whisky in the bottle. As with all innovations, there were no sound regulations for what should be stated on the label.

The "What is Whisky" question started after a 1905 court case in Islington, London over blended whisky and led to a Royal Commission in 1909 clearly specifying which drink could be called whisky and which one not. As a logical consequence brand owners would focus on giving more

information on the label, like the number of years the whisky had matured and a statement about the percentage of alcohol by volume (ABV).

Blended whisky brands far outnumbered single malt whisky. The latter simply used the distillery name to distinguish itself from the next one, but the blenders had to fiercely compete for a place on the shelves and on the eyeballs of the prospective customer. Some would use their family name, like Chivas, Johnnie Walker, Teachers, Dewars and Ballantine's, while others created names. Laphroaig for instance launched a blend called Islay Mist in 1928.

Throughout the 20th century almost every Scottish brand that managed to survive regularly changed the packaging design and with it the label. Designs were often taken from historical scenes or figures. Not so with Laphroaig, which always stuck to black-and-white typography, only adding 'Laphroaig-green' stripes, for certain bottlings, the silhouette of the distillery and, since 1994, the Royal Warrant. Its migration from the original labelling to the modern version can be witnessed by looking at the various bottles adorning this book in chronological order.

Each country where the brand is imported has its own set of rules and regulations. What can be done in one country is not allowed in another. In the USA for instance, after Repeal, all states drew up their own laws regarding manufacture, sales, labelling and distribution. Whereas most Laphroaig bottlings in Europe are filled at 0.7 litre, the USA insists on 0.75 litre and the label usually mentions 'proof' as well as ABV. So, your 10-year-old Laphroaig at 40% ABV would be '80 proof' in the USA.

Laphroaig does not have a bottling plant on-site. The mature whisky is bottled on the mainland and diluted to the required percentages of alcohol by volume with demineralised water. The percentages vary from 40% ABV for the standard 10-year-old to 48% for the Quarter Cask. Laphroaig's cask strength bottling varies from 55-57% ABV and is not diluted.

Many legendary limited bottlings have found their way to whisky lovers around the world, both issued by Laphroaig itself and by various independent bottlers, such as Gordon & MacPhail, Cadenhead and Signatory.

Over the decades Laphroaig has launched various official distillery bottlings that are not available anymore, apart from the odd bottle at a collector's. NAS is not a new thing: until the 1940s no age statement was mentioned on the label. The bottle depicted on page 188 could not be dated exactly but it is highly probable this one was launched in the 1930s or maybe even earlier. It is the oldest known distillery bottling of Laphroaig to date.

From the 1950s the standard bottling became a 10-year-old, bottled at 40% ABV as well as 43% ABV and 91.4 proof for the USA. The accompanying texts vary throughout the following decades as follows: Old Liqueur Scotch Whisky from the 1940s into the 1950s, Islay Malt Scotch Whisky from the 1960s into the 1970s, Unblended Islay Malt Scotch Whisky in the 1980s and Islay Single Malt Scotch Whisky from the 1990s until now.

Around 1985 the 15-year-old appeared, bottled at 43%. It turned out to be a very successful expression of Laphroaig, winning many awards. The first bottlings featured a big red '15' on the label, being replaced by normal text for later bottlings. The casks from 1978 and 1983 that were signed by Prince Charles (see page 94) were also bottled as 15-year-olds and auctioned for charity. In 2009 the standard 15-year-old was replaced by the 18-year-old, available until May 2015 when it was replaced by a new, limited, 15-year-old labelled 200th Anniversary Edition (see page 195).

During Robin Shields' reign the first festival bottling was introduced in 2003 – an 11-year-old at 40% ABV. As of 2004 the festival bottlings have been bottled at a much higher strength, above 50% ABV, all very limited editions and highly collectible now. The 2006 festival expression consisted of 600 bottles, to please more consumers.

From 2008 forward the festival bottling has been called Cairdeas, which is Gaelic for Friendship. It was distillery manager John Campbell's grandmother who came up with this very appropriate name. The number of bottles available in 2015 illustrates how popular the Cairdeas has become over the years: 2,500 9-litre cases, the equivalent of 32,000 bottles.

Another remarkable series is the Highgrove Editions – Prince Charles' own line of bottlings. The first one – a 1989 vintage - was launched in the early 2000s. All proceeds went to a charity chosen by HRH. Originally this expression sported a Laphroaig label, but that was replaced by a tailor-made Highgrove label. This 'private label' Laphroaig can be purchased in the Highgrove Shops in Tetbury (Gloucestershire) and London, as well as online.

The most famous vintage bottling, by many considered as one of, if not the best Laphroaig thus far is the 1974 31-year-old for La Maison du Whisky. Other famous bottlings are the 1980, 1981, 27-year-old and Cairdeas 30 year-old bottlings. The latter was opened at the eve of Feis Ile (as can be read on page 211).

Scandinavia has always had a unique bond with Laphroaig and received special limited bottlings for various years, only available in 'Viking Country'. From 2005 on many special bottlings found their way to a multitude of customers, often restricted to Tax Free Shops, such as the Laphroaig PX. All in all too many to mention here. Solid sources for further information about Laphroaig bottlings are The Legend of Laphroaig and www.laphroaigcollector.com.

## Meet Robert Hicks

At first choosing casks for bottling would have been the task of owner/distillery manager. Later on that task went to master blenders like Robert Hicks. He was responsible for most bottlings between 1992 and 2012. Employed by Laphroaig's parent company, not working exclusively at the distillery, he made an indelible stamp on the quality of Laphroaig.

He was born on 3 March 1945 and after his formal education he joined the whisky industry in 1964. Over time he acquired knowledge of all aspects of the industry from distilling, maturation and blending to bottling. In 1970 the Scottish division of Hiram Walker & Sons, then owner of Ballantine's, appointed Robert assistant blender. Eventually he became Master Blender for Allied Distillers and was responsible for many brands, among which Laphroaig and Teacher's, until his retirement. In November 2005 he started his own Scotch Whisky Consultancy and was asked by Beam Global UK Ltd. to become consultant Master Blender and Brand Ambassador for Laphroaig and other whiskies owned by Beam Global, a task he performed until 2012.

When once asked about the highlight in his career he mentioned Laphroaig receiving the first ever title Distillery of the Year in 1998 from the International Spirits Challenge. The honour befell the distillery again in 1999 and 2003. The awards, trophies and medals that can be credited in part to Robert's role as Master Blender are too numerous to describe in detail. One he is especially proud of is the San Francisco World Spirits Competition 2006 where Laphroaig 30 Year won the highest honour of "Best Whisky of Show" and a Double Gold medal. Laphroaig 10 Year, Laphroaig 10 Year Cask Strength, Laphroaig 15 Year and Laphroaig Quarter Cask all were Double Gold winners and Laphroaig was named as Distiller of the Year.

Developing many different expressions over the years, Laphroaig Cask Strength in 1994, the one he's most proud of was Laphroaig Quarter Cask in 2003 which, in the words of the Scotch Brand Director for Beam Global Sprits and Wines 'to produce this exciting and unique Laphroaig variant is a tribute to the skills of Robert Hicks, our Master Blender who has overseen every step of this unrivalled process'.

After his retirement Robert Hicks was awarded a Lifetime Achievement Award in London, in March 2006. For many years after he was a familiar face at many a whisky event throughout the world, conducting master classes and creating rumour around the brand. Laphroaig lovers thank many excellent bottlings to this remarkable man. Today John Campbell chooses the casks. He insists on being assisted by members of his crew, among whom Vicky Stevens and the warehouse men. They know their whisky intimately, spending everyday surrounded by thousands of casks.

## Core Range in 2015

## Duty Free in 2015

## Special Releases for the Bicentenary 1815-2015

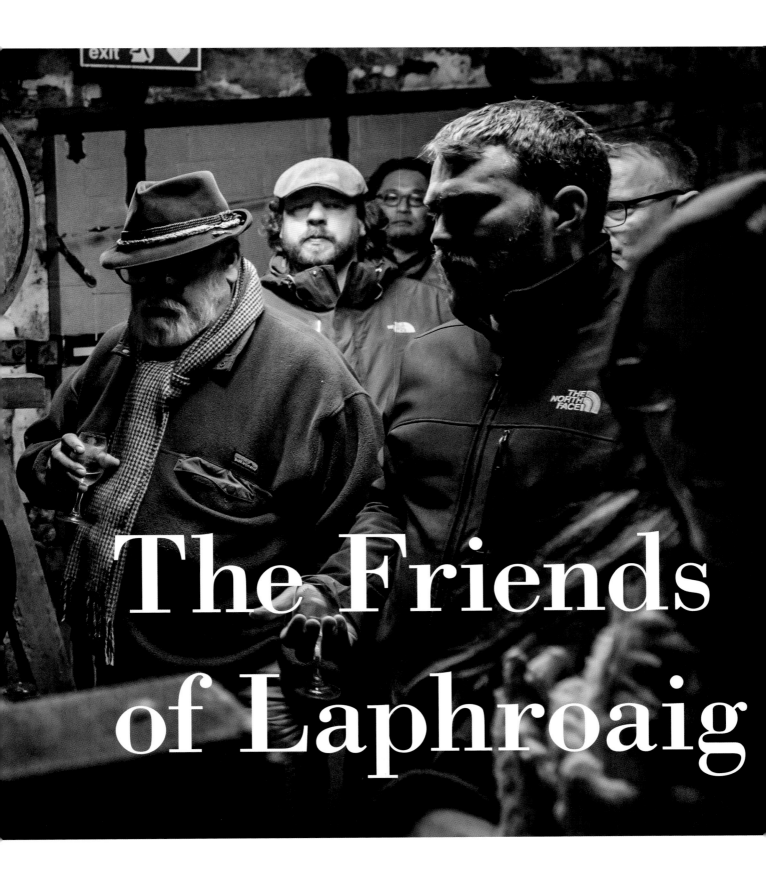

# The Friends
# of Laphroaig

# The Friends of Laphroaig

As of today more than 700,000 Friends of Laphroaig (FoL) worldwide 'own' a little piece of soil on Islay. They can come and visit, raise their national flag or conduct special services on their land, which is remarkable given the size of each plot (1 square foot). All Friends are given a certificate proving their lifetime lease on a numbered plot. The first 60,000 were registered in books available at the visitor centre; the following members have been recorded in an online register. Via the website they can order special products, such as limited bottlings and merchandise articles, made available only to Friends.

But being a Friend is much more than being the 'owner' of a tiny piece of Islay's soil. It is about being part of a worldwide community. A community that has grown out of an idea conceived in 1993, when a complimentary dram of Laphroaig was sent out to a select group of people. The mini bottle was accompanied by an invitation from Jeremy Weatherhead, Laphroaig's Brand Manager at the time, to become a Friend. The only thing you had to do was to fill in the enclosed card and return it to the distillery.

As a follow up, then-distillery manager Iain Henderson responded with special periodical newsletters. In the spring of 1994 he sent the first one we could find in the archives, announcing that the Friends program had been officially launched. Furthermore he proudly mentioned the upcoming visit of Prince Charles who would grant the distillery his Royal Warrant that year. An open day at Laphroaig celebrated the 500th anniversary of Scotch whisky production by present day methods and money was raised for the local primary school Gaelic choir. A copy of the Ileach was enclosed, in which issue the visit of HRH is duly reported.

HRH is officially a Friend of Laphroaig and the proud owner of plot number 1. The original format of finding your plot was to pace it out (before GPS). The starting point was on Royal soil: plot 1!!

Many letters to Friends would follow, often accompanied with a pre-postage paid card to encourage an existing Friend to invite a new Friend. All these letters from Iain can be seen as little time capsules of what happened on the island and at the distillery, apart from making Laphroaig. We've assembled some nuggets from days gone by and welded them into a timeline, without the pretence of being complete.

In the 21 years of its existence the FoL program has grown and become one of the most succesful brand loyalty programs in the world. Many wonderful comments and stories have been sent to Laphroaig by mail, email or on the FoL website, from members all over the world. We've made a random selection for you, having dug through 21 years of archives, both paper and digital. You can find them on the flyleafs of the book.

In the spring letter of 1995 Iain mentions one of HRH's casks being bottled and auctioned to raise money for the MacMillan Cancer Fund. He does not restrict himself to Laphroaig and informs FoL about the closure of Bruichladdich. Over 100 Friends have made a visit to the distillery.

The 1996 spring letter welcomes Friends in various European and Asian countries. Until then it was mainly people in England and Scotland who responded. Yoshino-san from Japan visited and cut his plot with nail scissors at Easter. He is invited back to cut the other 20,000 plots and is promised boots his own size next time. The famous 1976 vintage, chosen by Robert Hicks from 20 casks, is being released about the same time and is offered for ...£51.30 per bottle. Whoever kept it might sell it for up to £1,200 now, but we prefer to drink the stuff inside the bottle.

The Christmas letter that same year informs that 5,000 visitors had made the pilgrimage to Islay and 743 among them were Friends. Now 12 volumes of Friends Registers with 200 names per register are on display at the distillery. Iain mentions the closure of Ardbeg (a distillery he briefly ran alongside Laphroaig for Allied) and that Laphroaig offers a 30-year-old Ardbeg for sale. The two have always been closely connected, even celebrating their bicentenary in the same year. Included with the letter is a video 'Laphroaig: The History & Making of Laphroaig – No Half Measures' presented by Tony Hawks, of which a copy still exists in the distillery archives. 1996 also saw the launch of Laphroaig's website. Interested whisky lovers can sign up as a Friend online now, but there is no special Friends area on the site yet.

*Three descendants of Sir Ernest Shackleton and his team celebrate reaching the South Pole in 2009: Henry Worsley, Will Gow and Henry Adams.*

In the 1997 Spring letter, Friends read that tours can be made by appointment and are now regularly scheduled. Whoever wants to see the famous Registers, has to identify himself as a Friend. The coming of a book is announced, titled No Half Measures. It's a 48 page full-colour booklet, written by Graham Nown and will be sent to Friends who fill out a questionnaire and return it to the distillery.

The 1997 Christmas letter reveals a record-breaking year for visitors to Islay as well as Friends visits to the distillery, but does not mention exact figures, apart from £500 raised by the visitors for the local lifeboat station. The 30-year-old Laphroaig bottling now sells in the distillery store for £200 per bottle. The 'love-or-hate' theme is first mentioned, a phrase supposedly coined by the late Michael Jackson, don among the 20th century whisky writers. The logo would later appear in the shop as cuff links, among other merchandise.

The 1998 Spring and Christmas letters register 67,000 Friends of Laphroaig and the staggering growth of FoL at a rate of 400 per week. Of the 61 visitors during the Christmas shutdown, 51 are Friends. There is the new Gunners Bar in the maltings for them, which doubles as the shop, and a small museum area where people can wait to go on the next tour. The 15-year-old is temporarily on ration. A specially designed bookcase has been built to hold the FoL Registers.

1999 Spring letter: a new website is launched with a special area dedicated to the FoL. Now they can directly communicate with each other and are offered special prices for various items. A few bottles of the 15-year-old cask given to Prince Charles will be auctioned exclusively in the FoL section on the website. A special announcement is made to encourage new Friends to join. Whoever registers before November will be eligible to win a trip for two to Islay. Ten runners up will win a bottle of the 10-year-old.

1999 Christmas letter: John Campbell is introduced as Iain's 'new young assistant' as well as Margaret as a permanent tour guide. She is the wife of Donnie Stevenson, who has been employed by Laphroaig since 1994 and built the Gunner's Bar. Iain further mentions having been to the USA and meeting Friends there. The first marriage of two Friends at the distillery takes place in September that year. The turn of the century also marks the end of the written letters sent to the ever-growing FoL population. Instead, as of 2000 Iain will maintain a diary on the website. He invites Friends to send interesting stories about how they got acquainted with Laphroaig.

2000 – A major refurbishment in parts of the distillery. Iain writes in his diary that the first records of distilling on Islay go back 505 years. He thanks Friends for their continuing donations to the lifeboat fund. (As can be read in the history chapter, Bessie Williamson was a great philanthropist and always prepared to give money to the good cause. Doing things for charity has been ingrained in Laphroaig's DNA since). Iain asks Friends to email him when they cannot get access to the FoL site. For the first time a special Laphroaig calendar is available.

2001 – The 40-year-old is launched, a Laphroaig distilled from local Golden Promise barley during the reign of Bessie. The bottling comes from hoggies that were filled on 14 March 1960 and put to rest in Warehouse No. 1. They render 4,000 bottles, priced £375. Some 'characters' at the distillery are introduced by means of a special leaflet.

In 2002 Iain Henderson writes his retirement letter, stating: 'One of the things I will miss the most is meeting and spending time with Friends of Laphroaig. Learning where you come from, your interests, your first Laphroaig and so on. I'll also miss the unique camaraderie that I have with my fellow distillers on Islay. I will miss the guys and gals in the industry who have been part of my life as well.'

That year has been the busiest for visitors on Islay so far. During Feis Ile at least 1,000 visitors come to Laphroaig Day. Calmac is planning more ferry services for the future and Iain is looking for a successor. The FoL website counts over 10,000 visitors monthly. Iain is happy to see how many among them have built virtual homes on their plot and promises to make one final diary entry on the website.

Long time master blender Robert Hicks also sends a letter to Friends requesting that they all convey their best wishes to Iain via the website. These contributions will be collected in a special volume and for every message money will be donated to the Guide Dogs for the Blind Association. The donation will be made in Iain Henderson's name.

From then on the website and email are the main means of contact with the FoL community. Slowly but surely social media are embraced by Laphroaig as well as the various Friends. Streaming video had been introduced in 2007 when a live tasting, hosted by John Campbell together with Jim 'Whisky Bible' Murray was 'narrow casted' over the internet from London. There has been a live tasting at a different location each year since.

*Royal Visit 2008*

HRH Prince Charles visited Laphroaig 4 June 2008 as part of his 60th birthday celebrations. He tried his hand at turning the malt and received a copy of *The Legend of Laphroaig*. The 2008 live tasting edition took place on Islay with special guest Martine Nouet, aka The Queen of the Still. In 2009 it was held in Kentucky; in 2010 Jerez, Spain hosted the tasting. Sydney, Australia played host to the 2011 edition, where John Campbell and Robert Hicks were joined by Lin Johnston, the great-great-great-granddaughter of co-founder of Laphroaig, Alexander Johnston. Nuremberg, Germany organized the 2012 edition, followed by New York in 2013 and the island of Fjäderholmarna just off the coast of Stockholm, Sweden in 2014. The 2015 live tasting could not be held anywhere else than at the distillery, as part of the bicentenary celebration.

On the FoL section of Laphroaig's website many more stories can be found in the Writers Corner, which is divided into the following sections: Classic Moments, My First Laphroaig, Strangest Places and Laphroaig Cocktails & Recipes. Furthermore each Friend can download his plot certificate. And even view his plot from a satellite image. There is a virtual whisky shelf showing his favourite versions. The chat room is the virtual meeting place where questions can be asked and remarks left. A world map shows per country how many Friends reside there. Friends can also participate in a charity auction or enter a contest. Currently there are two. A monthly photo contest where Friends vote on other Friends submitted photos. The winner receives a FoL tartan scarf. The other one is a caption contest where Friends make a caption for a photo selected by Laphroaig. Other Friends vote for the best caption and the winner receives a Laphroaig glass. Via webcams installed in various places at the distillery, whisky lovers can virtually see Laphroaig being made.

Since the FoL website is under permanent development, new functionalities will show up over time. In the public section of its website Laphroaig encourages any visitor to leave a note, quoting Mark Twain who once said: 'The public is the only critic whose opinion is worth anything at all.'

*Lin Johnston 2011*

*Live tasting in Sweden 2014*

In 2012 a Tartan contest was offered, to mark the 18th anniversary of FoL.

*All Friends were asked to create a tartan and then other Friends voted on it. They had a 'tartan genera-*
*tor' on the site, so it was relatively easy to do. The winning designer got an entire kilt woven on Islay*
*in the FoL tartan. Currently the items available in that tartan are a woollen scarf made on Islay at the*
*woollen mill and a pin of wellies in the tartan. There have been numerous requests for kilts or wool to*
*be made available, but so far to no avail.*

*The winner of more than 8,000 entries was Patrick McCoy from the USA, holding plot number 367071,*
*who described his design as follows: The black, white, and green are the official Laphroaig colours.*
*The small blue strip represents the water that is so important to making the whisky. The light brown*
*represents the malted barley (which gives Laphroaig its signature taste) and also the finished whisky*
*itself, which is so dear to the hearts of all FoL.*

## The Visitor Centre

On Islay there is a saying; 'We don't make Friends easily but the ones we do are for life'. The ultimate place to meet Friends from other parts of the world in real life might be the visitor centre at the distillery.

A drop of the cratur at the place where it is made tastes even better than at home. The visitor centre and shop is run by Vicky Stevens, Manager and Emma Boyle, Assistant Manager. They are supported by six full time and two part time tour guides.

Along one of the walls in the cosy FoL lounge at the visitors centre, a large number of the famous leather Registers is on display. They contain names of Friends of Laphroaig from more than 150 countries.

There is a free dram at the bar for everybody of legal drinking age at the end of a tour. The hardcore and new fans of Laphroaig can purchase many of their favourite expressions and a wide range of merchandise

Behind the shop is a beautiful museum with artefacts of days gone by. On one wall a giant cupboard stands with paper flags of many nations: for Friends who come to mark their plot. They will be given a GPS tracker and the famous 'Laphroaig-green' wellies to aid in finding their square foot of Islay.

At the back of the museum is a solid wooden door, which gives access to a beautiful tasting room that can hold 24 people at a time. Attendees can sign a bung with their name and put it in a hole on the Opinions Welcome wall. When the spaces are all filled, the bungs are taken to the warehouse and used to seal casks. Then the wall is ready for a new batch. Over time many casks will have personalised bungs from Friends of Laphroaig.

## Special Friends of Laphroaig Events during the Bicentenary Celebration

These events took place throughout 2015. While the focus was on Feis Ile, there was also a beautiful cairn built with a time capsule, a Royal visit, a unique Laphroaig Live from the distillery, and special whiskies were released. These included a 15-year-old for the 200th anniversary, the 2015 Cairdeas, a 21-year-old for the 21st anniversary of the FOL, and a 32-year-old presented at Laphroaig Live in September. And of course, this book was launched to commemorate it all.

Feis Ile is the annual eight-day festival of food, whisky and music on Islay. Each day is customarily hosted by a different distillery. The 2015 edition was a special one, celebrating Laphroaig with all kinds of exclusive activities.

The Sunday evening before Laphroaig Day more than 100 Friends came together for 'This is Your Laphroaig' hosted by John Campbell and Simon Brooking. Together they presented three different drams of Laphroaig, paired with special canapés. The first whisky was a 30-year-old Cairdeas from the archives, chosen by three FOL from different countries as the best expression they ever tasted. Then the return of the 15-year-old was celebrated. Last but not least was the 2015 Cairdeas, created from barley exclusively malted at Laphroaig's own malting floors and distilled without using the Big Still. The dram was intended as a recreation of Laphroaig as it would have been made during the reign of Bessie Williamson.

On Tuesday 26 May 2015, Laphroaig Day, hundreds of Friends old and new came to take part in the birthday celebrations. Apart from the regular tours and plot visits, attendees could book special tastings, such as '200 Years of Laphroaig Going Back In Time'. This three hour tour took guests to the floor maltings, to an 'illicit' still and to the warehouses to show how things were done 100 and more years ago. A highlight for many was making their own personal blend of Laphroaig at the end of the tour.

John Campbell gave a heart-warming speech to celebrate 200 years of whisky making at Laphroaig and Angela Dunbar sang a birthday song for the hundreds gathered. The giant birthday cake was cut by longest serving employee James McGregor assisted by visitor centre assistant manager Emma Boyle, in front of the filling store. Live music and special tastings continued all day.

A brand new tasting room behind the museum was reserved for three unique tastings called 'The Making of' where we gave a glimpse behind the scenes of the making of *Laphroaig 1815-2015*. After the presentation each group assembled at a specific location at the distillery where their picture was taken for the book. Thus the fortunate few who obtained a ticket became an actual visual part of the history of Laphroaig. The three group pictures can be seen on the following two pages, accompanied by the names of the attendees.

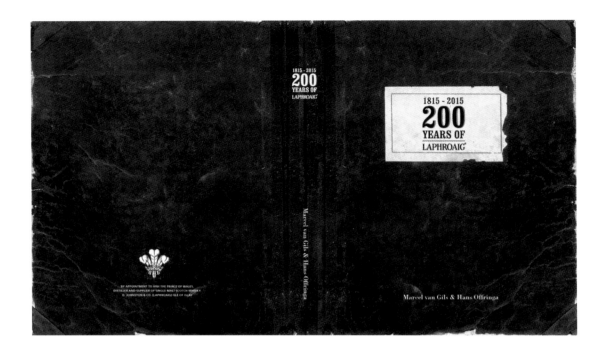

*Standing (left to right): Bino Gopal, Peter Notter, Daniela Huber Notter, Ronald Pfennigsdorf, Gudrun Pfennigsdorf, William Thomas, Kurt A. Maitland, Brittany Garrison, Karey Lucas-Hughes, Torbjörn Korssell, Martin Hughes, Jompa Cervin, Thomas Fehrm, Hans Perjos, Johnny Hellfritzsch. Kneeling (left to right): Joseph Howell, Matthew J. Lurin, William C. Meyers, Bo Jernberg, Ola Rosén, Karl Erim Eriksen, Reinhold Silh.*

Standing (left to right): Peter Altzar, Joanna McGarry, David McGarry, Andy Backhouse, Kari Urholm, Bruce Newsom, Karen Pashley, Tommy Svälas, Martyn Pashley, John Behrendt, Mikael Svälas. Kneeling (left to right): Jens Ritschewald, Glenis Reagon, Mikael Holst.

Standing (left to right): Graham MacKenney, Thomas Speller, Mark Diefenbach, Anurag Birla, Miles Constable, Angus MacRaild, Patrick E. Loyd, Lorraine Constable, Bram van Glabbeek, Iris Wanner, Kenneth Thieunke, Marco Azzoni, Paula Howse, Tim Howse, Flemming Hartøft, Preben Senniksen, Hans-Henrick Jorgensen. Seated (left to right): Ansgar Speller, Johanne McInnis, Dawn Knowles, Tom Knowles, Shaz Gilboa, Ofer Ben-Or, Rotem Ackermann.

## Royal Visit 26 June 2015

26 June 2015 HRH Prince Charles visited Laphroaig for the third time in 21 years as part of the bicentenary celebrations. He used his official Scottish title Duke of Rothesay and was hosted by John Campbell, Patrick Loudon McIain Stewart, Lord-Lieutenant of Argyll and Bute, Lady Lithgow, Deputy Lord-Lieutenant of Argyll and Bute, and Mick Ord, Director of Scotch and Irish Whiskies at Beam Suntory.

All 33 employees were present throughout the distillery so they could each have a chance to greet the Duke during his distillery tour where he filled, bunged and signed an ex-bourbon cask. He also officially opened the cairn in the FoL field by unveiling a special plaque and leading a toast with a dram of the limited edition 15-year-old. Inside the cairn is a time capsule, as well as space for Friends to have a wee dram.

This Royal visit also marked the launch of the Laphroaig Legacy Fund, a charitable initiative supporting the people, the community and the environment of Islay with local initiatives. Proceeds from the auction of a 40 year-old-bottle signed during the Duke's 2008 visit is designated for the Fund, as well as 1£ from each bottle of the limited edition 21-year-old and Cairdeas sold in 2015.

John Campbell remarked at the occasion: 'We are absolutely delighted to welcome the Duke back to Laphroaig to commemorate what is a momentous year for our distillery and brand. We are extremely grateful for his ongoing support over the years, which has helped enable us to preserve the unique heritage of the Scottish whisky industry and to give back to our community. Our 200th anniversary is an opportunity for us to continue to support the region through The Laphroaig Legacy Fund, celebrate our position as an integral part of the local economy, and help ensure that the community of Islay can prosper into the future.'

## Laphroaig Live 2015

On Thursday 24 September a selected group of distinguished guests from Beam Suntory and the Friends of Laphroaig joined the employees of Laphroaig for the annual Live Tasting. This event took place at the distillery floor maltings and was hosted by Murray Norton, former BBC radio and tv presenter and local politician on the island of Jersey. He was joined by distillery manager John Campbell, Scottish actor of *Outlander* fame Sam Heughan, editor of the respected Swedish magazine *Allt Om Whisky* Emma Andersson and German journalist, Master of the Quaich and IWSC judge Bernhard Schäfer.

Together they discussed and tasted the following drams: Laphroaig 15 Year Old, Laphroaig Cairdeas 2015, Laphroaig 21 Year Old and Laphroaig 32 Year Old, all four of them released to celebrate the bicentenary. This unique year warranted the much-lauded return of the 15 Year Old. The Cairdeas 2015 was made of malt exclusively from Laphroaig's floor maltings, distilled only in the small stills and matured in the No.1 Warehouse. The 21 Year Old was created in celebration of the Friends of Laphroaig coming of age. The 32 Year Old matured solely in ex-Oloroso sherry casks completed the tasting.

From New York City, Simon Brooking, Laphroaig's Master Ambassador in the USA, joined via a web connection and simultaneously tasted the same whiskies with his respected guests. The main audience was the enthusiastic community of Laphroaig fans who watched and participated live from around the world.


## Heritage

Five special guests were portrayed with John Campbell after the tasting had taken place, from left to right: Murdo Reed, Colin Ross, John McDougall, Iain Henderson and Denis Nicol. This re-markable fivesome consecutively managed Laphroaig from 1970 till 2002.

Together these fine men represent past, present and future of Laphroaig and an important part of Islay's distilling history. After all, it is the people who matter most!

Slàinte Mhath,

*Marcel van Gils and Hans Offringa*
*The Netherlands, November 2015*

# Acknowledgments

We would like to thank the following people, companies and institutions for their much appreciated time and help during the making of this book:

Tom Anderson Jr, Beam Suntory, Robin Brilleman, Simon Brooking, Elsa Davidson, Hans Dillesse, Hannah Fisher, Leonoor van Gils, Emma Goudie, Iain Henderson, Robert Hicks, Lin Johnston, Valerie Johnston-Macfarlane, Dr. Horst Klassen, Dr Jane Knowles, Sheila Kronenberger, Becky Lovett Offringa, John Macfarlane, Ian Macilwain, Charles MacLean, Angus MacRaild, Roger McWee, Chris Middleton, The Mitchell Library, Museum of Islay Life, Denis Nicol, National Archives of Scotland, National Library of Scotland, Martine Nouet, Finlay Payne, Helen Powell, Tim Puett, Janna Ramsay-Best, Eila Ramsay-Clapham, Bill Rankin (†), Murdo Reed, Colin Ross, Louis Reps, Iain Russell, Sukhinder Sing, Bill Scott, Laurien Stam, the crew of tall ship *Thalassa*, Phil Thompson, Simon Thompson, Archive Services of the University of Glasgow, VPH Digital, Calhoun Witham III. And last but not least: all the people at Laphroaig!

## SOURCES

*Archives*
The Church of Jesus Christ of Latter Day Saints
Glasgow University
Islay Census 1841-1901
Laphroaig Distillery
The Mitchell Library
Museum of Islay Life
National Archives of Scotland
National Library of Scotland
Old parish records Bowmore and Kildalton
The Royal Commission on the Ancient and Historical Monuments of Scotland (RCAHMS)
The Scottish Brewing Archive (SBA)
The State Library of South-Australia
The Victoria Library – National Archives of Australia
Whisky Magazine, Issues 1, 12, 34, 56, 60, 62.

*Books*
Barnard, Alfred, *The Whisky Distilleries of the United Kingdom*, 1887.
Barnard, Alfred, *How to Blend Scotch Whisky*, 1904.

Brilleman, Robin, *Islay, Whisky-eiland vol geschiedenis*, Whisky Informatie Centrum Nederland, 2010, ISBN 978 90 81305 426.

Gils, Marcel van and Hans Offringa, *The Legend of Laphroaig*, Still Publishing, 2007, ISBN 978 90 89100 276.

Lamont, W.D., *Ancient & Medieval Sculptured Stones of Islay*, John Smith, 1988.

MacLean, Charles, *Scotch Whisky, A Liquid History*, Cassell Illustrated, 2005, ISBN 194 4034 011.

Morrice, Philip, *The Whisky Distilleries of Scotland and Ireland*, Harper Publishing, 1987.

Moss, Michael S. and John R. Hume, *The Making of Scotch Whisky*, James & James, 1981, ISBN 090 7383 009.

Newton, Norman, *Islay*, Pevensey Press, 2001, ISBN 090 7115 90X.

Nown, Graham, *Laphroaig, No Half Measures*, Good Books Ltd, 1997, ISBN 094 6555 427.

Payne, Finlay Johnson, *The Maclans/Johnstons of Ardnamurchan, Islay and Canada*. F.J. Payne, 1998, ISBN 978 18 59332 160.

Ramsay, Freda, *The Day Book of Daniel Campbell of Shawfield 1776*, Aberdeen University Press, 1991, ISBN 008 0409 334.

Ramsay, Lucy ed., *The Stent Book and Acts of the Balliary of Islay 1718-1843*, British Library, 2011, ISBN 978 12 41045 357.

Russell, Iain, 'Elizabeth Leitch Williamson' in *Oxford Dictionary of National Biography*, Oxford University Press, 2004, ISBN 979 01 98614 111.

Smith, Gavin D. and John McDougall, *Worts, Worms and Washbacks*, NWP Ltd, 2003, ISBN 189 7784 651.

Storrie, Margaret, *Islay: Biography of an Island*, The OA Press, second edition, 1997, ISBN 090 7651 011.

Wilson, Neil, *The Island Whisky Trail*, NWP Ltd, 2003, ISBN 190 3238 498.

Wilson, Neil, *Scotch & Water*, NWP Ltd, 1998, ISBN 189 7784 589.

*Websites*

alchemywebsite.com

archive.scotsman.com

britishnewspaperarchive.co.uk

brynmawr.edu

celticmalts.com

copper-alembic.com

crystalinks.com

discovery.nationalarchives.gov.uk

greydragon.org

islayinfo.com

laphroaig.com

laphroaigcollector.com

nasgov.uk

scotlandspeople.gov.uk

© 2015 Conceptual Continuity

First edition

ISBN 978-90-78668-31-2


**Concept & Text** Hans Offringa

**Contributing Editor** Marcel van Gils


**Research** Marcel van Gils and Hans Offringa

**Research Management** Becky Lovett Offringa


**Contemporary Photography**

Marcel van Gils: front flyleaf, pages 2, 4, 8-9, 28-29, 36-37, 89, 95, 98, 99, 101, 103, 104, 106-107, 109, 110-111, 113, 116 r, 117 r, 125, 126-127, 128, 129, 130, 132-133, 135, 138, 140, 142, 144, 146, 148-149, 150, 152, 154-155, 156, 158, 160, 162-163, 164, 166, 168, 170, 173, 174, 177, 178, 181, 182, 185, 190 l, 196-197, 199, 200, 202-203, 205, 210, 212, 213, 214-215, 222-223. Photography Assistant: Leonoor van Gils.


**Contributed Photography**

Hans Offringa: pages 11, 13, 18-19, 23, 24-25, 114, 118-119, 121, 122-123, 136-137, 193; Guus Pauka: pages 50, 58, 60, 65, 83, 186-187, 188, 190 r, 191; Sukhinder Singh p.63; John McDougall p.73; Dr. Horst Klassen pp. 78, 79, 80, 81; Colin Ross p.92; Robin Shields p.97; Robert Hicks p.192; Islay Studios p.206; Jalle Fotograf p.207; Dominic Loneragan p.207; Paul Block p.208; James Deane: back flyleaf.


**Archive Illustrations and Photography** Glasgow University and Laphroaig Distillery


**Photo Editing** Marcel van Gils and Laurien Stam

**Text Editing** Becky Lovett Offringa

**Design and Layout** Laurien Stam

**Printing** Grafistar

## South Africa

'In response to the slogan competition in Top of the Times, I suggest:
**_Laphroaig – Single Malt, Double Enjoyment, Triple Crown._**
You understand that the prize of a year's supply of
Laphroaig whetted my incentive.'

## USA

'I have a mental image of property owners in size
12 Wellingtons and lifebelts carrying anchors,
dodging low flying geese.
**_It must make a man mighty thirsty._**'

## India

'India does not allow the import of any kind of alcohol for trade.
Passengers to the country are allowed one litre of spirits.
For Friends like us, this is the only route to get our requirements.
**_You can well imagine the pleasure on receiving any
of these treasured bottles._**'